Mastering
Deputy Headship

LEADERSHIP SKILLS IN EDUCATION MANAGEMENT

Series Editor: Professor Trevor Kerry

Forthcoming titles:

From Teacher to Middle Manager
Making the Next Step
by Susan Tranter

The Head Teacher in the 21st Century
Being a Successful School Leader
by Frank Green

The Special Educational Needs Coordinator
Maximising Your Potential
by Vic Shuttleworth

Mastering
Deputy Headship

Acquiring the skills for future leadership

Professor Trevor Kerry

PEARSON EDUCATION LIMITED

Edinburgh Gate
Harlow CM20 2JE
Tel: +44 (0)1279 623623
Fax: +44 (0)1279 431059

Website: www.pearsoned.co.uk

First published in Great Britain in 2000

ISBN 0 273 64927 2

British Library Cataloguing in Publication Data
A CIP catalogue record of this book can be obtained from the British Library.

10 9 8

Typeset by Boyd Elliott Typesetting
Printed by Bell and Bain Ltd., Glasgow

The Publishers' policy is to use paper manufactured from sustainable forests.

About the author

TREVOR KERRY is Professor of Education and Vice-President of the College of Teachers, and Visiting Professor in the International Educational Leadership Centre, University of Lincolnshire and Humberside. He holds an MA in education management from the Open University, and MPhil and PhD degrees in education from Nottingham University.

Trevor's fundamental interest is in effective teaching. He was research officer with two national projects on teaching methods: the Teacher Education Project (1976–1980) funded by the DES, and the Developing Pupils' Thinking Project (1981–1983) for the Schools' Council. He has taught in primary, secondary, further and higher education, and held posts in initial and in-service teacher education. His most recent roles have been as Principal Lecturer in Educational Research at Charlotte Mason College; Head of Department and Pro-Principal at Doncaster College of Further & Higher Education; Senior General Adviser (INSET & FE) with Norfolk LEA; and Staff Tutor for education in the East Midlands Region for the Open University. Until recently he was also the part-time special needs co-ordinator at a primary school in Lincolnshire. He has written over 100 journal articles, and written and edited more than two dozen books, and has taught students pursuing higher degrees in education management at MSc, MBA, EdD and PhD levels.

Professor Kerry has been engaged in the Schools for the Future Project at the Lincoln University campus. In this role he has written extensively on the five-term year and other time-related issues in school management. He is well known in this field as a consultant and lecturer and – with his wife, Carolle – he runs TK Consultancy offering in-service training to schools in the areas of teaching skills such as questioning and educating the more able.

Contents

Series editor's introduction

The nature of schools and the educative process is changing. Indications are that the first decade of the twenty-first century will see the fastest, and the most far-reaching, changes in schools and schooling since the compulsory education system was established. The signs are there if we have eyes to see them:

■ advances in technology will alter the nature of learning. While school has been characterised by the need for groups of people to assemble together to listen to a teacher, the computer, its software and the Internet are making learning accessible to anyone, according to need and inclination, without their having to come together;

■ technology, through the computer and through video-conferencing, gives access on a local level to global opportunities. If they have the technology, pupils in Britain can access the very best lessons and the very best teachers from anywhere in the world. In place of thousands of teachers teaching thousands of different, more or less good, lessons on a topic, the student will be able to access the most complete and dynamic lesson regardless of where it is taught;

■ computers even threaten the concept of school time. Since the computer gives access at unlimited times and in unlimited places, learning need no longer be associated with time slots at all;

■ but it is not just computers that are driving the forces of education into new channels. Economics plays a part. School buildings are inflexible and costly, yet they often remain unused for more than 80 per cent of the time – during vacations, evenings, nights and so on. Costly plant lying idle is a luxury that society may feel unable to afford;

■ increasingly, we can see non-teachers of various kinds becoming more central to the education process. There was a time when no adult but a teacher would have been found in a classroom. Now schools often have a greater complement of technicians, administrators, nursery assistants, special needs assistants, students from care courses, voluntary helpers and counsellors than they do of teaching staff.

So key areas – how learning takes place, where it takes place, when, its quality, the type of plant required, the nature of the people who deliver it – are all in the melting pot as we enter the new millennium. If ever there was a moment for developing a new breed of educational leaders who could span the effective management of the present system and forge a path into the future, this is it.

This series is therefore dedicated to achieving those ends: to help education managers at various levels in the system to become the leaders now and the pioneers of the future. The titles are all written by people with proven track records of innovation. The style is intended to be direct, and the reader is asked to engage with the text in order to maximise the training benefit that the books can deliver.

Change is rarely comfortable, but it can be exciting. This series hopes to communicate to school leaders something of the confidence that is needed to manage change, and something of the fulfilment that comes from meeting challenge successfully.

Professor Trevor Kerry

List of tasks

List of tables

List of figures

Preface

The readers of this book will be deputies in post and those aspiring to a deputy headship in both the primary and secondary sectors.

The book begins with the assumption that the reader is applying for a deputy's post, but moves quickly to examine carefully the tasks that are expected of deputies in post. Thus, whether already appointed or seeking appointment, the reader will be guided to the necessary skills for the job. Indeed, the book would be invaluable reading in preparation for a job interview for a deputy headship, as well as being a manual of practice for a practising deputy.

A glance at a sample of advertisements for posts as deputies in just one edition of the *Times Educational Supplement* gives a clue to why such a book is important.

Job 1 requires someone:

- who has high expectations of pupil behaviour and achievement
- who demonstrates excellent organisational and interpersonal skills
- who has the ability to manage a leading role in curriculum development.

Job 2 needs:

- high expectations of children's learning
- a positive, caring attitude, enthusiasm and a sense of humour
- ability to inspire, lead and motivate
- commitment to partnership working with the head, parents and governors.

Job 3 puts a further gloss on the role in demanding someone who:

- is an excellent classroom practitioner with a successful track record in their subject
- is energetic in working individually or as part of a team
- can bring the best out of colleagues.

The intention of this book is to help you become such a paragon!

Acknowledgements

The part played by many deputies in compiling the material in this book is gratefully acknowledged. In particular, Mandy Wilding, a Vice President of the College of Teachers, provided a significant amount of information. Other deputies and senior staff who helped included Sally-Ann Evans, Rob Ridout and Graham Sharpe. Many other deputies in primary and secondary schools were observed going about their daily tasks – often unaware that their approaches to their roles were of interest to the author. Their comments, too, were a great boon. Carolle Kerry provided much of the material on the governors' perspectives.

Since this book is based on the collected wisdom of so many deputies and others in primary and secondary schools across the country, the plural pronoun (we) is used throughout.

How to use this book

This is a book about the skills required of a deputy head in a primary or secondary school. The book uses a variety of means to set out, examine and exemplify these skills:

- text – to provide information, discussion and continuity
- tables and figures – to convey data quickly or in graphic form
- lists – to set out key issues or skills
- tasks – to involve the reader in practice
- case studies – to provide real examples of management/leadership situations.

The book can be used in a variety of ways. It can be read as a textbook: the reader will then simply read over, but not carry out, the Tasks. It can be used as a source book: you can consult the relevant sections (such as Chairing meetings or Public speaking) as the need arises. It can be used as a training manual by an individual, in which case you will work through it systematically, pausing to carry out each Task as you come to it. Finally, the book can be used as a training manual for a course on the role of the deputy. To get the most from the book, we would recommend that you use the Tasks and keep a log of the outcomes from them.

The book is based on the philosophy that effective managers need specific skills for the job. These skills can be identified, analysed, refined, broken down into subskills, taught, learned and even assessed. We hope that the book will be seen by busy deputies as a kind of *vade-mecum* – a source of comfort and inspiration. It would be useful, too, as the basis of a systematic dialogue between a deputy and a mentor.

This book stresses the importance of the links between the practice of being a deputy and the appropriate management theory that underpins specific aspects of the role. We believe that practice without theory is a house built on sand; and that theory without translation into sound practice is an empty vessel.

We trust that this manual of skills, based as it is on grounded theory and experience, will bridge the gap that often exists for deputies: between proceeding in the job on the basis of instinct but without proper training and accessing training that addresses the really practical issues that arise in schools.

Starting off

Introduction

Every new job is a challenge, but becoming a deputy head in either a primary or secondary school may be one of the most challenging steps an aspiring teacher can take.

This is reflected in the vocabulary of deputy headship. Here are some of the typical words and descriptions taken from reports and articles about being a deputy, published over recent months:

conflict

torn

balancing act

mission impossible

tensions

challenging

difficult.

This book attempts to help those who wish to become deputies, or who have recently started down that career path, to cope better.

Being a deputy is almost by definition a conflict role. The deputy stands between two clearly defined groups – the staff and the head. It is a position fraught with ambiguity. Indeed, unlike headship, it is a role embarked on by many with little preparation and with even less training. This book draws on the experiences of those who are, and have been, deputies in order to throw some light on the skills and practice that enable the role to be handled with dexterity and success. It is also a text that actively seeks models and examples from management theory to explain and illuminate the processes of management and leadership in schools at this specific level of responsibility.

The book uses a blend of reflective advice, case study, practical activities and observation of practice to help the reader engage with the function of being the deputy head. All of the material is based on fact, but names, genders and settings have been changed, and insights from several incidents may be combined to form fresh scenarios through which learning from the text can take place. In this way we hope to present readable and valid learning experiences without in any sense writing an autobiography of personal experiences or case histories of particular schools. We have drawn on the freely donated time and concern of many deputies of our acquaintance to help us compile this material.

The book assumes that you are intending to apply for a deputy head's post or newly arrived in one. The practical activities address the reader in this assumed context.

When we embarked on writing this book, we contemplated writing separate texts for primary and secondary deputies. But our researches soon showed that, while contexts may vary slightly, the same principles apply in both situations. Shared concerns accounted for more than 90 per cent of the planned material, and so we decided to compile a single volume, with examples drawn from each phase.

In this first chapter we deal with the things that deputies might do before and while seeking an appointment but before taking up a post, and we look at the first few hours in the job.

Preparation

How much preparation do deputies have for their new role?

'Not a lot,' might seem a fair answer. Typically, a secondary deputy will come into post after a successful career as a classroom teacher followed by a period in middle management, as a head of a subject department or as a pastoral manager. For primary deputies it is quite possible that previous experience will involve classroom teaching combined with a co-ordination role (perhaps of several subjects!), but there may be less formal 'middle management' experience because primary schools are smaller and less hierarchical than secondary schools.

We will start by looking at some of the career paths that may have led to the momentous day on which appointment to deputy headship is made.

An important first step, if you have not yet obtained a deputy's post, is to examine your career profile and try to assess the strengths and weaknesses revealed in it. The pro forma included in Task 1 may help you do this.

TASK 1

Reviewing your career to date

Use the questions in this pro forma to look at your career to date, and to try to identify the strengths you can bring to the role of deputy. It is also important to note those qualities or experiences that you lack, and to begin to establish a strategy for making good any deficiency. You can turn this pro forma into a 'running log' of your progress by updating it on a regular basis as you achieve your targets.

1 What academic/professional qualifications do you hold – in subjects, in teaching and in management theory and practice?

2 What posts have you held in the profession to date? In each case, log the types and levels of responsibilities you have had.

3 Think through your current and previous posts and identify what you consider to be your achievements.

4 Try to make some assessment of your personality, how you come over to colleagues. What do you perceive to be your strengths?

5 By reviewing your answers to questions 1–4, try to write down the kinds of managerial/leadership skills you think you have:

- people skills

- administrative skills

- planning skills and creative approaches

- time-management skills

- financial and resource-control skills

- external relations and marketing skills

- others (add to the list …).

6 Now draw together all your answers into a brief statement of what you feel you could offer a school if you were to be appointed (or have recently been appointed) as a deputy.

7 So what is missing from your profile? What qualifications, experiences, skills and personality traits do you need to develop?

8 Make a plan for upgrading your calibre as a deputy by tackling the items you have identified in your answer to question 7.

Task 1 will have helped you carry out some self-assessment. We all learn about the roles we undertake, or aspire to undertake, in a variety of ways. The following paragraphs list some of the opportunities for learning and note their strengths and shortcomings.

Learning from experience: Most new deputies will have had a small taste of a management role in school prior to appointment. What almost all of them say is that this experience does *not* fit them for their new role. The co-ordinator or head of department is clearly 'one of us' (the teachers), not 'one of them' (the managers). Leading a subject to which one's colleagues are fundamentally committed does not generally generate much conflict. It is a 'first among equals' role, described best in warm adjectives of togetherness and shared vision. Teamwork rules. You may lead by example, and may have to carry a larger than average share of the team's burden, but you are appreciated all the more for this by your colleagues. The transition to the role of deputy brings with it another culture (more of this later).

Learning the theory: Some new deputies, prior to seeking an appointment to the role, will have tried to equip themselves by undertaking systematic study of management theory. Usually this is in the form of a master's degree course or a management diploma – a half-way house to the degree – or through some route such as the National Professional Qualification for Headship (NPQH) offered by the government. New deputies who had pursued this course of action told us that it was useful in that it made them reflect on their management practice. What courses cannot do is to equip the student for every practical problem that may arise. Those who had not been down this road did feel at a disadvantage in the new role, because they had little except their own limited experience on which to draw when things started to happen in the new job.

Role modelling: All new deputies had had experience of watching other deputies at work, and most had consciously observed these colleagues when they themselves had become interested in promotion. Some role models were negative ('I wouldn't follow in Blogg's footsteps') while others were very positive ('Jane was a real star: just the right blend of firmness and tact – I want to be like her, though I don't think I'll ever be that good'). However, new deputies soon had to face two very significant facts. First, their personality was not the same as that of their role model. Second, the circumstances and relationships of one school are never replicated in another. Having a role model (better still, role models) is useful, in a very generalised way, but it can never be a blueprint for personal success.

Formal preparation: In a few cases, individual aspirants to deputy headship were groomed by their current heads and given special responsibilities in their present school so they could practise their skills before applying for a deputy's post. This worked well enough in large secondary schools, but was rather divisive in smaller primary settings. Any leadership experience has some value (and it could equally well be gained outside school, in an office or through responsibility attached to a leisure pursuit), and it is more comforting to make mistakes in a situation that one is about to leave than in one that is about to be joined.

The interview: 'The day of the interview is a bit of a blur'; 'You are totally preoccupied with the interview process'. The interview experience – sometimes well planned to show candidates over the plant and let them speak to a range of potential future colleagues – may not be useful as part of the preparation of the successful candidate for the new post.

Post-appointment familiarisation: Once appointed, the appointee would do well to spend some time in the school. Our new deputies spoke of problems obtaining release to do this. When they did visit, they wanted to spend most time observing the daily systems of the new school and getting a feel for the kinds of teaching across the school. The two crucial issues that need attention from the outset seem to be:

- non-contact time, and

- mentor support.

In primary schools it is common for deputies not to have non-contact time, or for this to be very limited. Our secondary deputies pointed out how much they appreciated the 'thinking time' that non-contact time gave them, and found this a very liberating aspect of taking up a new post as deputy. Non-contact time is an issue that should be clarified at interview for primary deputies; there ought, after all, to be some payback for the extra work they are called on to do. All new deputies wanted to feel that there were support mechanisms for them in the early days of the new post; mentoring by a senior colleague could provide this security. An independent mentor (a deputy or head in another school, for example, or someone from a local HE management department) might be more appropriate than one in the deputy's own school. Again, this is a matter that ought to be negotiable at the appointment stage.

Now would be a good time to assess the influences that are shaping your preparations for, and attitudes towards, deputy headship by tackling Task 2.

TASK 2

Examining your preparations for the role

Look back over each of the six headings above. Use the pro forma below to reflect on how each of these relates to your current experience.

Learning from experience:
(E.g. what management/leadership experiences have you had in school/out of school? What are the main lessons that you have gained from them?)

Learning theory:
(E.g. what do you know about management theory? What have you done/do you plan to do to reflect more systematically on management processes?)

Role modelling:
(E.g. who are your positive role models? What have you learned from them? What have you learned from negative role models? Why are these lessons important? How do you differ from your role models?)

Formal preparation:
(E.g. have you had, or can you negotiate, any activities or situations that may help you prepare for a leadership role?)

The interview:
(There is always an opportunity at interview to ask questions. What would you want to know about your new school? If you were given a chance to look around for half a day before the interview, what would you hope to see and what issues would you want to explore?)

Post-appointment familiarisation (if applicable at this stage)*:*
(E.g. what forms of induction and support can you expect/request? What are the values and limitations of this provision?)

Tasks 1 and 2 have helped you assess your readiness for deputy headship. In the rest of the book we shall be moving on to examine the role itself and what happens to new deputies when they move into post. As you progress through the book you will be asked to scrutinise in more detail many of the essential skills that have been hinted at in these opening pages.

The first morning

Going to work on the first day of a new job can be daunting, but when the job is a high-profile one such as that of deputy it can be even more so! Our deputies were concerned with image. Men and women wanted to be:

■ professional

■ early

■ apparently relaxed

- smart
- cheerful
- the epitome of efficiency
- well prepared for their classroom teaching
- as familiar as possible with the new school and its layout.

Tuning in your psyche to a new context is an important part of the process of settling successfully into a new role. Taking things slowly, acting in a measured way and presenting an impression of confidence are all important. Give the whole process some time and thought in the days preceding the event, and plan quite deliberately.

This is the morning, of all mornings, when you don't want the car to break down (call a taxi and go back for it later?), nor for you to fall down the stairs (don't hurry?), rip your clothes on a nail (take some spares?), or forget anything (make a list and keep checking it?).

First encounters

Every teacher knows the importance of meeting a new class for the first time: precedents are set that are hard to break down later if all does not go according to plan (*see* Chapter 3). The same principle applies to the first day in a new management role. The short case study that follows was taken from a new deputy's diary.

CASE STUDY

The first day

I arrived at school at 7.45 am expecting to be the first there, only to discover that mine was the fifth car in the carpark. Was this symptomatic of the first day of term or was it a sign of a highly committed and dedicated staff?

I felt apprehensive as I entered the school building and found my designated classroom. Before long, the teacher of the parallel class came in to wish me luck and talk through the day. Shortly after this the head of KS1 came in to welcome me and offer her assistance, if required. Throughout the day various members of staff approached me to offer words of welcome or support. I valued their positive moves and I began to warm towards the staff who had taken the trouble to talk to me.

Conversely, there were some staff who viewed me warily and avoided all contact. At times, I sensed that staff members were talking about me. This made me feel uncomfortable even though I felt their comments could be positive as well as negative. As a staff manager I had to expect that staff would talk about me – and not always favourably – but it was still disturbing.

The head reacted brightly and cheerfully towards me. She made sure that she was in the staffroom at break times and she sat and had her lunch with me in the dining hall. She was friendly and approachable, but gave me the space during the school day to get to know my class, without interruption. The head knew that staff and parents would watch me closely and so it was important to establish good relationships with my class as a priority. Therefore, I was determined to learn the children's names quickly.

However, things happened rapidly. Even before the start of the school day I had a few curious children and parents sneaking into school to catch a first glimpse of me and if possible to exchange a few words. One parent asked so many questions in the space of several minutes that I felt trapped into disclosing personal information. Afterwards I was annoyed with myself that I had failed to sidestep her inquisition. I had made a conscious decision that I would tread quietly and keep my distance, giving as few personal details about myself as possible, at least until I knew people better.

This extract from a deputy's reflective log reveals just some of the insecurities of being in the new post. A more specific issue is coming from a familiar situation into one that is wholly unfamiliar.

Coping with being de-skilled

Two of our colleagues wrote:

One of the things I found most difficult was learning the new school routines. As I had taken up my post mid-year I was the only new member of staff. Everyone else, including the children, knew the ropes. I found it difficult to disassociate my pervading feelings of inadequacy from the fact that since I was new I could not be expected to know the school's procedures. I hated having to ask where children line up, where the toilets were and what happens in assembly.

I knew that I had to operate now outside my subject area. In the latter I felt secure; but now I had to find out about, and empathise with, people whose subjects and approaches were different from mine. Initially, I felt vulnerable about this.

It is difficult to cope with being de-skilled. It is as well to prepare yourself mentally for this, though you will try your best to find answers to as many questions as you can before you arrive at your new job. But even when you arrive as well prepared as you can be, you may still encounter tests of your character and resourcefulness.

———— Being put to the test by colleagues ————

Most of our deputies felt that they had been 'tested' by their new colleagues very early on in their new role. This is both challenging and frightening. Below are two short case studies of being put to the test, both of which happened very early on. One is a primary example and one secondary.

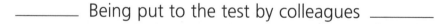

CASE STUDY

Changing the lining up procedures in a primary school

Changes in school procedures and customs can be difficult to implement, as this new deputy discovered. In this incident resistance to change is explored.

In discussion with the headteacher about health and safety in school, the new deputy, Chris, raised his concerns about playground procedures. The infant and junior playgrounds are on two different levels and access between them is via a slope. At the end of break there was severe congestion on the top junior playground due to year 2 lining up with the juniors. There were ten classes on one playground and four classes on the other. Therefore, the head and deputy raised the issue of congestion at the weekly senior management team (SMT) meeting. The existing arrangements were discussed and Chris proposed that if the year 2 children lined up with KS1 there would be a better balance of numbers. There were no objections to Chris's suggestions.

The proposal was carried forward to the next staff meeting, with Chris explaining the rationale for the change. Staff appeared to acknowledge the problems. However, a number of objections were put forward and the discussions became quite heated. Arguments were based on the following:

1 Year 2 were allowed to play in the junior area and would therefore have to be moved down to the infant playground. This would involve extra time and supervisory duties. (Who was going to be responsible?)

2 The proposed movement of children could create behavioural problems and an even greater safety hazard due to the slope, e.g. pushing, shoving.

3 The time slippage was largely due to staff arriving late to collect their classes. It was felt that this could improve if staff were punctual. The staff proposed that they would all improve their timekeeping to see if this would resolve the situation.

There was a temporary improvement as staff made an effort to collect their classes on time. However, this was short-lived and Chris remained dissatisfied with the arrangements. At the end of his first term he informed the heads of KS1 and KS2 that his initial proposal for change in the system of lining up would be implemented at the start of the new term. He agreed the essential support and supervision to enable a smooth transition to the new system.

CASE STUDY

Having an instant opinion in a secondary school

On the first day I was in the school, a man appeared at my door. I asked him, very politely, what I could do to help. To this he replied:

'Tell me what you think about Information and Communications Technology in the school.'

I had never met this person before, and the question made me catch my breath. I managed to think quickly enough to say that I wasn't entirely sure at this stage, having only been in the school for a few hours.

However, I did go on to indicate that I would be making myself familiar with ICT in the school, and also with the school's intentions and targets for ICT. I felt this was a bit of a 'cop-out', but then I asked him who he was.

It turned out that he was the Head of ICT.

When you have read the case studies, attempt Task 3.

TASK 3

Coping with the first crisis

Choose either the primary or the secondary case study above. Read over the chosen case study again. Try to determine what went right and what went wrong in the situation.

If you choose the primary case study

In particular, consider the response of the three main parties to the proposals for change:

- the SMT
- the deputy, Chris
- the staff.

Now consider:

- the reason that the SMT might not have identified at its meeting the problems raised by staff
- any measures that Chris could have taken to avoid the conflict
- why staff were obstructive although they were prepared to accept the problem.

Finally, try to construct a diagram to show the sequence of change you would want to engineer in order to resolve this incident.

If you choose the secondary case study

What do you think was the motivation for the head of department's question and the mode of delivering it?

How well did the new deputy cope with the situation?

What lessons do you suppose the new deputy learned about dealing with colleagues?

What steps might he have taken to prevent this kind of situation happening again?

Coping strategies for the first day and first week

We asked a deputy to reflect on how best to cope with the early days in the role. What follows is a transcript of her response:

> *Think about the basic routines that you will expect to encounter in these early days. Make sure you understand the timings and protocols of the school. You are likely to get better information from support staff like the school secretary, bursar, caretaker and ancillaries than from the head (who may be too busy).*

Do not plan to be too ambitious in your own teaching in the first few days – there will be time to impress later! But keep the work interesting – you mustn't lose the students' confidence. Make sure all your resources are prepared and organised so that you can appear in public looking relaxed.

There seems to be a narrow path to tread between being so efficient that the staff around you feel inadequate or threatened, and showing you are competent and deserve their respect. You have to signal that you value their expertise, too.

Make arrangements to go out with a friend who is not part of the new school structure, but who will be willing to listen to your moans and frustrations. The first few days can be very lonely and it is important to establish your own network through which to sustain your relationships and support.

Linking theory to practice

So far in this chapter we have considered some of the initial qualities and skills that a deputy needs in order to demonstrate an ability to manage or lead. We have used the two concepts – management and leadership – as if they were interchangeable. It will be the last time we use the words in this way, because in reality they are rather different skills. To establish exactly why this is so we need to introduce briefly some theoretical underpinning (the issue is revisited in Chapter 5).

Managers and leaders serve different functions for any institution, be it a school or a major commercial enterprise.

Managers are the people who are concerned with the processes and procedures of the institution, with whether its day-to-day routines run efficiently and whether there are established practices, understood by all, that operate to ensure the smooth functioning of the institution. The manager is, in this sense, the servant of the organisation, running a tight ship behind the scenes, to ensure that everything proceeds smoothly. An efficient manager might well have a low public profile. He or she makes sure that the school's targets are achieved through co-ordinating the efforts of colleagues.

Leaders provide vision and the driving force to see that vision begin to become reality. They are target setters: creatives who produce ideas and inspire enthusiasm and loyalty as factors in improving performance. They are often quite high-profile people, who may be less worried about the details of systems and procedures provided that the overall vision is achieved.

Leadership has the following characteristics:

- it is a subset of management skills;
- it is about innovation and change;
- it is about teamwork to achieve the change;
- it is highly creative;
- it is about inspiring others rather than carrying out an executive function.

Members of a senior management team need to share between them the functions of both the leader and the manager. These functions can be divided between a number of individuals, provided that they are all carried out. Any one person can play both managerial and leadership roles.

Each school operates its managerial and leadership roles differently. All the following scenarios are common enough:

- in a secondary school, the deputy who spends almost all his/her energy on timetabling and cover arrangements, along with other administrative duties (management);
- in a primary school, the head who takes on all the administrative functions (management) but leaves curriculum innovation (leadership) to others;
- in any phase, the deputy or head who provides dynamic leadership so that the school is frequently in the news for all the right reasons – they may spend quite some time out of the institution talking to others about their creative ideas.

The role of a deputy is one in which it is almost always essential to provide elements of both management and leadership to the school and to the senior management team. This is just one of the many pressures inherent in the deputy's role. It is about tackling that role with the widest possible range of skills that the rest of this book is concerned.

—————— Summary ——————

Our intention is that, at the end of this chapter, you will have:

- reviewed your career and assessed the extent to which it has prepared you for the role of the deputy head
- considered your personal approaches to the role
- thought about the crucial first morning of the new appointment
- prepared yourself mentally for the first few days in the role
- started to consider the differences between leadership and management in schools.

chapter two

Working relationships with the headteacher

Establishing trust

The secret of a successful working relationship between a deputy and the headteacher is summed up in three words: trust, trust and trust.

This is the view of every deputy to whom we have spoken, though in practice it is important to understand that trust in this sense is made up of a number of factors. It is with these factors that this chapter is concerned.

The newly appointed deputy may face a number of problems in feeling that a relationship is being established. The following case study identifies some of the issues.

CASE STUDY

Establishing trust between the deputy and the head

The deputy quoted here is very much aware of the need to establish trust at two levels: with the head, but also with the other staff.

I was very conscious of wanting to convey an image of myself as a reflective, enthusiastic and knowledgeable person to my head. In retrospect, I could have held back slightly on my keenness. The most important way in which I gained trust during the first few weeks was through being flexible and supportive. An example of this: the head always does a playground duty at 8.45. If the head was tied up with a problem, or a parent, I was very quick to offer to cover (this also served the purpose of me being seen by, and having contact with, parents). I made sure I was around during the lunchtime, whereas all the other staff were very protective of their lunchtime entitlement. I think the fact that I kept a smile on my face was most welcome (especially as Ofsted was imminent). I have tried to remain open and supportive in my relationship with the head. We are both aware of the tension that if I am seen to support the head's view too wholeheartedly, decisions then start to become an issue of 'management vs staff'.

A newly appointed deputy is establishing both trust and a personal relationship and rapport with the head. Task 4 asks you to think about this in a little more detail.

TASK 4

Establishing or improving rapport with the head

Re-read the case study above.

What strategies are recorded there for helping to build a relationship between the deputy and the head?

Evaluate these strategies as they might apply in your own situation. What would work, what would not work and what else could you do?

Strategies identified here are largely informal (possibly spontaneous and unplanned). But what about more formal strategies: planned meetings, discussing issues and policies? What part might these play?

Identify one strategy that you have not tried before. Put it into practice. Did it work? What was successful/unsuccessful about it?

———— Trust and communication ————

Part of the business of building trust is about communication. In successful working relations between deputies and heads, communication was seen as a factor in that success. For example, the following quotation summarises the views of deputies in Hertfordshire and is taken from an important piece of research conducted in the county:

It was obvious that these successful partnerships were sustained by the two sharing their ideas, knowledge of what was going on in the school and what they thought about initiatives and plans. All of them [i.e. heads and their deputies] clearly talked to each other a great deal. Much of this dialogue was face to face but they sometimes phoned one another, used school intercoms or wrote one

cont.

> *another memos ... Most organized formal meetings between themselves when they could regularly update each other and share perceptions and concerns.*
>
> 'It's good to talk', *Primary School Manager*, Issue 6, Sept/Oct 1995, pp. 7–10.

While both formal and informal communication played their part in these partnerships, in some cases the deputy and head also developed a deeper understanding. They were able to read one another's body language and each developed a kind of sixth sense about the other's reactions. Such a relationship takes a little time to build. The level of formal contact was variable, and depended to a large extent on the degree to which the deputy was timetabled to teach students.

 Developing a vision

The key to understanding the value of communication probably lies in the development of a shared vision for the school. Although formal planning has a place in the management of a school, and is required for some purposes of accountability, it is becoming increasingly recognised that the real issue is not the production of plans but the generation of visions. Having a strategic vision – where does the school need to be in one year/three years/five years? – gives a degree of flexibility (in how to achieve the goals) that a plan does not. (There is more on defining the vision in Chapter 9.)

The discussion of the vision and philosophy for the school is a fruitful area for developing communication and understanding between a deputy and the head. It becomes not only a sharing process, but a learning process: a genuinely collegiate act, and a platform on which effective management and leadership can be mounted. It is, in itself, supportive, relieving the isolation that a management role often brings. Something of the flavour of this point is evident in the following brief extract from a deputy's log:

> *During the Ofsted inspection the head was obviously feeling very isolated. She was being interviewed by the inspectors about aspects of the school, but in other ways could only stand back and watch the staff getting on with their teaching. Though I was quite preoccupied myself (as a teacher and in my role as deputy) with the inspection process, I made time to compare notes with her and to listen to her perceptions of what was happening ...*

Of course, not all deputy/head partnerships begin well or progress smoothly all the time. One of the 'downsides' for a new deputy coming into a school that has a fairly well-established staff, many of whom may have worked with the head for a significant time, is that it is the deputy who will feel like an outsider. It is precisely in these circumstances that communication and trust may break down. The next case study describes just such a situation.

CASE STUDY

Negative relationships

One member of staff had been particularly unhelpful. Though the incidents were, of themselves, quite trivial, there was a determination by Richard that he would not conform to management decisions and school procedures. When I was forced to challenge him he was surly and even rude.

I then discovered, by accident, that the head had held a meeting with two middle managers about my relations with Richard. I felt very threatened by this, and allowed my feelings to show in treating the middle managers very coolly. My position seemed to have been undermined. Eventually, my resentment led me to open the issue with the head, though she had not spoken of it.

The head defended her action in speaking about me without my presence. She claimed that she could not have invited me to a meeting at which I was being discussed. But she was, she said, assured as a result of the meeting that Richard was behaving unreasonably. She had, therefore, spoken to him to spell out the need for him both to conform to the school's requirements and to treat me with proper courtesy.

It was certainly true that Richard had become, as a result, both more conformist and also more polite in a very formal way.

On reflection, I am pleased that the head dealt with the problem of Richard. But I still feel threatened in the way in which she chose to go about it. The two middle managers are long-standing members of staff, and the head trusts their judgements. I am not convinced yet that she trusts mine!

I still feel that too many people got involved in this incident, and that there was an element of 'listening to staffroom gossip' on the head's part.

The matters described in the case study are not very elevating. However, it is often possible to learn a great deal from situations that go wrong. The trick is to discover how to prevent them happening again. For this reason you should now attempt Task 5.

TASK 5

Losing confidence

Look back over the incident described in this case study. Try to assess what was right and what was wrong about the head's actions.

Examine the feelings of the deputy both during and after the event. How justified were they?

What could the deputy have done about this situation:

- to stop it developing as it did?
- to have sorted out the problem with the head?
- to have put matters on a better footing in terms of relations with the head?

If you are currently a deputy, have you had any similar experiences? How did you handle them?

Factors in partnership

Perhaps this is a good moment to reflect on the positive factors that condition and control good working relationships between deputies and heads.

From a deputy's perspective, these might include:

- a climate of honesty
- the ability to speak freely
- the capacity to try out ideas in a secure setting before implementation
- the freedom to operate in the role without constant supervision
- an awareness of support from above
- the option to disagree
- sharing knowledge about the school on all fronts
- professional behaviour at all times as a model for teacher–teacher relations
- time available for reflective discussion
- fair continuous appraisal – praise for things well done, guidance for improved performance.

The head might look in return for:

- personal support and encouragement in professional matters

- public support on issues concerning the vision for the school
- unbiased advice
- enthusiasm and commitment for the good of the school
- a colleague who relieves the head of some agreed management tasks to provide him/her with a chance to undertake personal thinking 'towards the vision' for the school
- collegial approaches to issues such as devising school policy
- reliability
- sensitivity as a channel of communication between the head and the staff.

Models of deputy headship

These considerations lead on to trying to review what this chapter has said or implied about models of deputy headship. The first model might be labelled 'Piggy in the middle':

MODEL 1

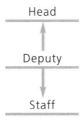

In Model 1 the deputy is torn between loyalty to the staff and loyalty to the head. One of our deputies warned against such a model:

> *Make no mistake about it. Once you cross the boundary to become a deputy, you can no longer look upon yourself as one of the troops. Your loyalty is firmly with the head and the management team. Any attempt to be a go-between is doomed to failure, because the staff will know that you are a manager really, and the head may think of you as disloyal. Of course, you can represent the views of staff to the head, but you can never again be one of them.*

Model 2 sees the deputy as simply the mouthpiece of the head. This might be called the 'Chain of command' model:

MODEL 2

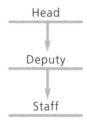

Head

Deputy

Staff

In Model 2 the head may become an almost irrelevant figure in the school, with all the real power vested in the deputy. An LEA adviser described this model as follows:

> *We were not surprised that Bogbrush school failed its Ofsted inspection and was put on special measures. Nor that eventually it had to close. The head had been a passenger for years. He sometimes took phone calls. But he arrived before any staff or students, left after them, and in between remained firmly anchored in his study defended by a secretary who guarded the door like Cerberus. That, of course, was on the days he was not away at a course, a conference or some other external event.*

TASK 6

Devising other models of deputy/head relationships

Using Models 1 and 2, think about any other models you have seen or experienced for the ways in which deputies and heads relate to one another.

List and sketch out the models, and divide them into negative and positive models.

Now use the exercise to identify your preferred model of deputy/head working relationships.

_____ Summary _____

Our intention is that, at the end of this chapter, you will have:

■ reflected on the importance of trust between the deputy and the head
teacher

■ understood the role of developing, with other staff, a vision for the
school

■ examined some models of communication for deputy heads.

Roles deputies play

In our discussions with deputy heads it quickly became clear how many different roles they played. In this chapter we attempt an overview of what might be described as the 'top 15' roles. Other significant roles are dealt with throughout the book. But one early word of warning is, perhaps, in order here.

Job description

Among our deputies we found considerable variation with respect to job descriptions. Some had very full job descriptions, with some quite detailed specifications about what might form the targets for the deputy to achieve within the school. Others had minimal job descriptions couched in the most general of terms. The latter often included very 'trivial' activities. For example, we found one deputy in a further education institution whose role included organising the bus queues outside the building when students went back to their villages each evening. Another complained:

> *I was excluded from the annual budget planning.*

A further complaint among our deputies was that some general teaching duties conflicted with the time-consuming deputy role:

> *In comparison with the classroom teacher, the time before school, at breaks and at lunchtimes is clogged with management activity: working with support staff, being available to parents, attending working groups. What suffer are classroom preparation, and the things like putting up attractive displays. I can't get on to the photocopier ...*

Later in the chapter we give three examples of job descriptions to show the variation and to get you to think about this aspect of your role as deputy. For the moment we concentrate on the 15 'key roles'.

The 15 key roles for deputy heads

As a deputy you will be called on to play any, probably all, of the following key roles:

curriculum controller

pastoral manager

administrator

substitute head

timetabler

troubleshooter

diplomat

co-ordinator

executive officer

role model

disciplinarian

public relations officer

go-between

thinker

teacher.

This chapter spends a little time considering each of the key roles, and suggests some initial strategies that you might have to acquire in order to tackle, or prepare to tackle, each one.

Curriculum controller

In schools where there is more than one deputy, such as larger secondary schools, each deputy probably takes a specialist role: either as an administrator, or as a pastoral head, or as the curriculum guru. However, the trend in recent years, and in the primary sector (because one appointee has to fulfil all the roles), is for deputies to share or trade aspects of the total role, to be responsible for specific tasks and their outcomes rather than for an area of responsibility. It is probable that all deputies will need to take a curriculum lead at some stage in their time in post. Indeed, one of the things that secondary deputies said to us, which they shared with the primary sector to an extent, was the vulnerability they felt in having to be 'expert' in the complete range of curriculum areas.

While acknowledging the real fear here, it is perhaps important to emphasise that this is really a misunderstanding. The curriculum controller does not need to be, indeed cannot be, an expert on everything from IT to fabric design. The deputy draws on the expertise of those who are charged with curriculum control at the middle management level: the subject co-ordinators and heads of department. The deputy as curriculum controller needs two basic sets of skills:

- sufficient overall understanding of the individual subjects and their teaching within the school system to be able to judge the soundness of the advice being given by the middle managers;

- a grasp of the principles of whole curriculum building: what the curriculum of the school must legally achieve, what the policies of the school require it to achieve, what it would like to achieve (to fulfil the school's vision and mission statement) and how curriculum implementation works.

In itself this is a pretty tall order. Some of the skills (the law, policies) are a matter of reading and homework; but translating intentions into actions requires a wider range of skills and abilities. Some of these are dealt with later in this chapter and throughout the book.

TASK 7

Equipping yourself for curriculum management

How would you equip yourself with the practical knowledge you might need about the curriculum in the school in order for you to carry out a co-ordination role?

What would you need to know about individual subjects?

What would you need to ascertain about the school's vision for its whole curriculum?

How would you gain an impression of the delivery of the curriculum across both subjects and the age range of the students for whom you cater?

Make yourself two lists, using the pro forma below. In the left-hand column jot down what you need to know; and in the right-hand column note how you are going to acquire the information.

	Information needed	Means to acquire it
1		
2		
3		
4		
5		

Finally in this activity, put your plan into action and try to discover the information.

Pastoral manager

Another key role assigned to the deputy in many schools is that of the pastoral manager. Indeed, we have come across a number of schools where this is the main role of (one of) the deputies. In one such school (a small secondary school serving the fringe of a suburban population and some outlying villages) detailed research into the role was undertaken. From this it was possible to deduce the wide range of responsibilities held by this individual deputy (*see* Table 3.1). These specific responsibilities were, in turn, able to be broken down into job operations: in an interview with her, some 55 separate job operations carried out by the pastoral deputy were identified (Table 3.2). These two tables demonstrate the complexity of the role, and also the point that was made earlier, that carrying out a function may involve both very high- and very low-level tasks.

TABLE 3.1 The role of a pastoral deputy

1 Pastoral manager.

2 Head of a subject department.

3 Member of a senior management team.

4 Chair of pastoral teams.

5 Staff trainer.

6 Trainer for student teachers.

7 Organiser for parents' evenings.

8 Manager of the prefect system.

9 Co-ordinator of the option choice for older students.

10 Designated child abuse officer.

TABLE 3.2 Job operations performed by a pastoral deputy

1 Unlock fifth-year common room.

2 Answer queries from staff.

3 Answer queries from students.

4 Deal with correspondence and memos.

5 Attend senior management team meetings.

6 Keep discipline in assembly.

7 Take assembly.

8 Teach.

9 Organise exam work in own subject.

10 Teach beyond the school day.

11 Cover for absent colleagues.

12 Brief other staff on pastoral matters.

13 Report pastoral team decisions to SMT.

14 Counsel students.

15 Monitor students' option choices.

16 Keep records on students.

17 Chair pastoral committee and subcommittees.

18 Prepare agendas.

19 Keep minutes.

20 Publish minutes.

21 Prepare reports for governors.

22 Report periodically to the head.

23 Attend daily staff meetings.

24 Solicit information about students from staff.

25 Receive telephone calls.

26 Pass on information to staff about individual students.

27 Organise parents' evenings.

28 Brief the caretaker.

29 Attend Parent–Teacher Association (PTA) meetings.

30 Liaise with PTA officers.

31 Organise the refreshments for PTA and parents' events.

32 Organise the annual prize evening.

33 Write references for students.

34 Liaise with non-teaching professionals.

35 Call case conferences.

36 Attend case conferences.

37 Act as primary/secondary liaison officer.

38 Train other staff in pastoral care.

39 Act as designated officer for child abuse.

40 Attend pastoral training events.

41 Attend in-service training in own subject.

42 Call on external assistance: doctor, nurse, social services.

43 Deal with minor disciplinary offences.

44 Deal with serious disciplinary offences (including home visits).

45 Select prefects.

46 Train prefects.

47 Mark class work.

48 Keep records of attainment.

49 Liaise with local initial training (ITT) providers.

50 Organise provision for student teachers.

51 Brief initial trainees about the school.

52 Brief mentors for ITT students.

53 Observe ITT students at work.

54 Report on ITT students.

55 Support and advise ITT students.

Administrator

A third arm of the deputy's work is to act as a senior administrator. This function has tended to change in recent years. In the past, deputies were used to balance the school's books, to keep records and deal with paperwork. Increasingly, the paperwork is dealt with by secretarial staff and the financial matters have become the province of bursars. This is less true in the primary sector, and least true in the smallest of schools, but it is a fair generalisation.

Administrative functions now may involve the management of the personnel – the secretarial staff and bursars – who carry out these functions, but they still demand a knowledge of what to do with the outcomes of the work of these employees. Thus, the process of reflection on the implications of a school's balance sheet for the running of the school may be the task of a deputy. A deficit of £20 000 in the school budget may mean the loss of a staff member, or some alternative saving may need to be engineered.

The deputy head may be closely involved in, or responsible for, drawing up contingency plans – and it will be an onerous task. Another administrative task that often attaches to the deputy is that of organising the timetable, which is dealt with separately below.

Substitute head

Deputies may often have to act on the head's behalf. The changing nature of schools means that heads increasingly have to play a role in the local community. They are often absent from the school premises: at meetings with LEA staff or school sponsors, with business community representatives and so on. If the school is successful they may be in demand by the local teacher training institution to give talks, or they may be called away to national conferences as participants or speakers.

There are many legitimate reasons for a modern head to leave the school during the school day, and then the deputy has a role in covering the head's absence. At first, this may seem a daunting possibility; certainly, the deputy needs to know where the head is and how to make contact for advice. Time and experience will ease the problem of insecurity, though it is important for the head/deputy team to have clear policies for how matters might be handled in the head's absence. There is nothing more disruptive to an institution or its staff than to have a deputy pursuing a different policy when the head is away from that applying when the head is present.

Timetabler

One very specific duty of some deputy heads is to manage the timetable, and associated arrangements such as cover for staff absence. In a book of this length it is not possible to convey the various ways in which a school timetable might be constructed. These are often the topic of specialist courses, and aspiring deputies would do well to take advantage of such opportunities, even if timetable construction is not the pinnacle of their ambitions! But it is possible here to establish some basic principles and attitudes that can be helpful.

In a recent article in an Australian journal aimed at school principals, Michael Bradley (1999) makes the following points:

> There is no such thing as the tyranny of the timetable. There is, however, a people tyranny in which ... traditional timetablers make invalid assumptions about what a timetable is, and is not, capable of achieving. The timetable should be viewed as a liberating tool within which staff are able to juggle the competing demands of students, rooming, curriculum and limited resources to the benefit of students ... a fluid and flexible instrument rather than a restraint on one's imagination or on the programs available to students. The timetable should be an instrument of opportunity. (p. 2)

In the same journal another contributor, Mike Middleton, notes that timetables for schools are changing. In a report of his own small-scale research, 61 per cent of respondents said that their schools had altered school programmes to make better use of technology. In addition, 60 per cent of respondents had abandoned 'short' lessons in favour of longer sessions (more than 45 and sometimes beyond 80 minutes); 35 per cent had introduced a flexible school day; and 34 per cent had introduced school-based resource centres in which students could undertake project work or personal study.

Similar issues are affecting British schools. Initiatives such as flexible school days, learning centres, the five-term year and multitracking are becoming part of the British educational scene. Schools that offer community education inevitably need different kinds of timetables from traditional schools. The mechanisms of constructing a timetable can be learned; the attitudes that underpin the process are of considerably more importance and need to be engendered at an early stage in the deputy head's career.

Troubleshooter

One of the more disconcerting aspects of being a manager is that people expect to be able to call on you at a moment's notice, and find it entirely reasonable that you should be able to solve problems that they cannot. The deputy is often the person who can be found or is available when a disciplinary incident arises, or when an irate parent arrives just after the final bell for the day has gone.

One of the best ways of heading off this kind of problem is to anticipate it. Some of the very best deputies seem to have the knack of being on the corridors immediately before school or at break time; the disciplinary incident may never happen if this is the case. In the same way, the primary deputy who is obviously present at the start of a school day may pass a word or two with a concerned mum or dad that will alleviate a later problem. Being in the right place at the right time is an instinctive thing: there is no training course in that particular knack. Yet some school managers do seem to develop it, and it pays dividends.

Diplomat

Diplomacy is an art form; it is certainly not just compromise. Diplomacy suggests that a problem situation achieves a solution that is shared by, and acceptable to, all parties, and that this end product comes about as a result of some covert ability of the diplomatist to find the right path, use *le mot juste*, convey the right signals through body language, and show neither favouritism to one of the parties nor irritation at them both. Compromise, on the other hand, usually means that neither party is happy and that the manager has fallen short of achieving his or her real intentions.

Perhaps some readers will feel that, in a book of this kind, it is inappropriate to suggest that something as intangible as personality counts, and still less that such a desirable personality can be developed in some way. Yet we believe that both statements are true. One manager of our acquaintance tells this story:

> I was appointed to a new institution where I was a complete unknown, but where the staff had been together for a long time. When situations arose that needed some kind of resolution of an actual or potential conflict, I tried my level best to keep calm and to ask for a full – and frank – expression of opinion before testing the waters with a possible solution. I was, however, increasingly aware that my actions were provoking a negative atmosphere. One morning a middle manager came to me with a complaint. She was an intelligent person, a good teacher and a doctoral graduate. I asked her to sit down and talk me through the problem. I asked her what kind of outcome she would like to see from it. I put before her some alternative strategies from which she could select a solution that she could accept. As she got up to go I said: 'You are still not happy are you?' She turned and looked at me. 'You're right', she said. 'Then can I ask why not?' I said diffidently. 'Well', she said, after a pause: 'It's like this. Our previous manager used to shout and bawl us out. We knew where we stood with him. All this careful evaluation of effective solutions freaks us out. We'd rather be shouted at!'

God forbid we ever resort to bawling staff out as a managerial ploy! But what this cautionary tale tells us is this: as well as educating ourselves in professional behaviour for managers, we may have to educate our staff in being able to benefit from our professionalism.

Co-ordinator

Of all the people in the school, it is the deputy who probably does most to make sure that all the strands come together into a coherent whole – who is the archetypal co-ordinator. The deputy is like the conductor of an orchestra. The head (along with the governors) writes the music of policy, vision and intention. The deputy head brings together the disparate players and their instruments to turn the inert notes on the page into living harmony of performance: the students, the teachers, the non-teaching support staff, the administrators and the caretakers; the behaviour, the examination results; the day-to-day organisation of the school, the specialist provision, the resources, and the appropriate environment for learning – all of them working together to the same ends and in the same time.

Executive officer

At times, however, the tasks of the deputy can be construed through another metaphor: that of the executive officer. An executive carries out tasks in ways (according to policies) that have been determined by others. At times the deputy plays just this role. He or she is charged with implementing the policies of the school as agreed by the head, the governors and the formal meetings of the organisation. If the head wants students to follow a particular dress code, the deputy may be delegated to enforce it. If the governors decide that standards should rise by 5 per cent in SATs or GCSEs, the deputy may be required to oversee the processes that may bring this about. If the staff meeting agrees that a particular speaker is required for a training event, the deputy may be asked to arrange this.

In all these instances, the deputy is carrying out policy or decisions as an executive rather than forming the policy as a leader. It is important in undertaking the role effectively that deputies understand the role in which they are acting at any given time and can alter their behaviour accordingly.

Role model

The deputy's own conduct is always under scrutiny. At one level the deputy sets the tone for inter-staff personal and professional relations (more is said about this in a later chapter). At another level, the deputy's behaviour is seen as a measure of the tone of the school. One deputy wrote in his log:

> It had been the turn of our school to organise the district sports meeting. Very few teaching staff were willing to help with the refereeing, and at the end they left and there was almost no one to clear up the mess. So I set to, and tidied all the equipment and picked up the litter. One of the support staff who had helped out during the evening later complemented me to the head on 'getting my hands dirty and leading from the front'. It was nice that somebody noticed.

Disciplinarian

Some deputies have to take responsibility, to a large degree, for discipline around the school and for that of students generally. Here, deputies have to meet the expectations of students (to be firm but fair), of teachers (to support them) and of parents (to treat their children with respect).

Public relations officer

All good deputy heads are public relations officers for the school in the most generalised sense, but there may also be a more formal element to the role. In general, one might expect the head to play a significant part in representing the school to the wider community. However, so important are issues of public relations that head and deputy will probably have to share aspects of the task. This task may, for example, include all or any of the following:

- seeing current parents
- talking to prospective parents
- interviewing prospective students
- keeping tabs on the progress of former students
- producing promotional material such as school brochures
- briefing the press and photographers
- meeting other professionals: doctors, nurses, social workers, welfare officers, police officers, museums' officials, school suppliers
- dealing with governors – briefing them, hosting their visits
- meeting officials from 'twin towns'
- putting on public events (parents' evenings, concerts)
- liaising with local traders.

The list can be endless. These tasks require personal skills, tact, diplomacy, perhaps some familiarity with public speaking, visual skills, design skills and so on. While it is possible to get support from staff or outside professionals for some aspects of public relations – such as brochure design – this is very expensive. The days of school hospitality consisting of a broken chair in the corner of an untidy staffroom with a cup of dubious coffee in a stained mug are no longer appropriate in a competitive environment. These public relations tasks fall mainly to the head and the deputy to carry through with professionalism.

Go-between

Another role that causes some headaches for most deputy heads is that of go-between, by which we mean the difficult task of representing the head to the staff and the staff to the head. Almost every deputy to whom we spoke was aware of the tensions in this role. The point has been made that a deputy is firmly in the management camp and cannot lose sight of that. Nevertheless, it remains true that every conscientious deputy will want to reflect loyal support of the head to the staff, and also signal to the head something of the feelings of staff members concerning any controversial matter in the school.

This is not so much shuttle diplomacy as the ability to act as a channel of communication. The amount of success with which these twin roles can be achieved probably depends on the degree of trust between the deputy and the head, as we have discussed in Chapter 2.

Thinker

The role of the deputy head is one of the busiest, if not the busiest, in the school. We have all known deputies who have been so conscientiously employed in the minutiae of their jobs that they have been unable to detach themselves from these activities in order to think through the wider issues of education. This cannot be acceptable. The deputy is a leading professional, in many cases a 'head in waiting'. He or she must develop the capacity both to think through educational issues with vision and clarity, and to manufacture the opportunities for this thinking to take place.

One of the problems with Rodin's famous statue of 'The Thinker' is that it seems to imply that thinking can happen only when the thinker is in passive mode and relieved of other, e.g. physical, activity. Modern professional life is too short for such a luxury. The virtue of thinking is that it can be done *at the same time as* other, rather mundane things. Thinking can take place very appropriately during the washing up, while mowing the lawn, in the car wash, on buses or trains, and at many other 'marginal' times. What is needed is the mindset that says: I have a problem; I'll let it bubble away on the back burner for an hour or two; then I'll work over it systematically while I am ironing my shirts. Some of the deputy's most productive professional activity can thus be channelled in such a way that it doesn't 'take up time' in any conventional sense at all.

On the other hand, some 'thinking' tasks are time consuming and rely on the presence and participation of colleagues. Such a task is described in the short case study that follows.

CASE STUDY

A fulfilling role for a deputy

One of my roles is as staff development manager, which means that I have to compile the School Development Plan. The process involves:

- leading the review of the previous year's SDP

- noting key issues unfulfilled from this

- collecting and collating staff views about priorities and concerns

- liaising with the head to draw up a draft document

- presenting the draft to the staff for comment and amendment

- presenting the proposed plan to the governors.

There are a number of reasons why I feel this is a challenging and worthwhile task for me as a deputy:

- it lends credence to my role with the rest of the staff, as I am seen to be leading a significant area of the school's management

- it allows me to extend my overview of the school, the issues and needs of staff, students and parents

- it gives me a basis for engaging in dialogue with staff from all phases

- it gives me an arena in which to demonstrate my own skills and, hopefully, gain the trust and respect of colleagues

- it is intellectually stimulating and therefore provides intrinsic satisfaction.

Teacher

Finally in this review of the 'top 15' roles for deputy heads is the role of the deputy as a teacher. This role has been left until last *not* because it is the least important, but because it can then be given its proper prominence. All of our deputy heads agreed that:

- as a deputy, you are a 'lead teacher'

- as a lead teacher, staff look to your lessons to be of a high standard

- personal competence as a classroom practitioner raises your status in the eyes of colleagues

- high status as a teacher makes your leadership task easier.

But deputies have special problems. They often have too little classroom remission to carry out their deputy headship functions. There is a danger of stealing classroom time for management, with serious consequences for your classes. This leads to exactly the opposite outcome from the desired one described above.

Deputies, therefore, have to reassure themselves when they take on the role that these issues have been addressed within the job description and the organisation of the role that is proposed when the job is advertised, offered and accepted. Before acceptance there may be room for negotiation, even in the more constrained primary sector. But even once in post, the management role of a deputy may change, with knock-on effects on the classroom performance of the post holder. A renegotiation of roles and time allowances with the head and/or the governing body may be appropriate from time to time. Indeed, the best schools probably arrange an annual review, perhaps as part of appraisal.

_____ The job description revisited _____

This last point leads neatly back to where this chapter began: job descriptions.

It is unfortunate to have to introduce a rather pessimistic note here, but the plain fact is that, in practice, many deputies find that their job descriptions are less than adequate and that they are often 'dogsbodies'. This is true of both the primary and the secondary sector. Some researchers have described the deputy as 'weighed down by petty tasks' (Harrison and Gill, 1992), and Lowe (1998) called them 'the bolt-on appendage'. Though these remarks were directed at the primary sector, we all know of deputies in the secondary field who are confined to a turret room manipulating timetables or are limited to purely administrative tasks.

Hopefully, however, during your reading of this chapter you will have given a lot of thought to the job of the deputy: its range and potential for improving your school and developing your own abilities. In what follows you will find a Task to complete that focuses your attention on your job description (or on potential job descriptions if you are still seeking a post as a deputy head).

TASK 8

Revisiting your (potential) job description

Tables 3.3, 3.4 and 3.5 set out three job descriptions of varying quality for deputy head posts.

Read over the three descriptions, comparing and contrasting them. Make some notes about their respective strengths and weaknesses.

If you have a job description of your own, compare this with the other three and make notes similarly.

Now reflect on what your ideal job description (for your current post, or for your desired post) would contain. These headings might help you:

- essential elements

- desirable elements

- additional preferred elements.

TABLE 3.3 Job description 1 – Primary deputy

I have no job description. There was none published for the role. The original advert contained vague phrases like 'supporting the head teacher' and 'overseeing non-teaching staff', but that was all. I've never been given anything else.

TABLE 3.4 Job description 2 – Secondary deputy

- to be the point of referral for Pastoral, Curriculum Leaders and staff

- to monitor the teaching and learning across the curriculum including pastoral curriculum

- to ensure that the curriculum is delivered effectively

- to ensure the efficient deployment of staff

- to have oversight of the timetable team

- to maintain and develop assessment, recording and reporting strategies to assist teaching and learning and to enable appropriate targets to be set

- to keep abreast of educational developments related to the above

- to assist with the day to day running of the school

- to work with the Governors of the school.

TABLE 3.5 Job description 3 – Secondary deputy

The deputy will:

- be comfortable about working in an inner city

- share the school's commitment to sporting achievement

- have proven management experience

- have a record of success in raising attainment

- be committed to working in a challenging environment

- be ambitious to pursue his/her own professional development

- be involved in managing the school's access arrangement and bus service for pupils

- be a practising Christian

- substitute for the head as required.

————— Summary —————

Our intention is that, at the end of this chapter, you will have:

- scrutinised your job description

- analysed some job roles

- reflected on the range of tasks (and, therefore, skills) that you need as a deputy head

- improved your understanding of the role and perhaps also your job description itself.

Relations with other staff

At the beginning of this book we noted that conflict was one of the dimensions of the deputy head's role. The deputy stands between the school's senior management and the rank-and-file members of staff, both teaching and non-teaching. It is not surprising, therefore, that many of the incidents that deputies described to us as happening to them early in their careers in the role were about these relationships.

Let us begin the chapter by looking at a case study of a typical incident. When you have read the case study carefully, tackle Task 9.

CASE STUDY

Dimensions of space, ownership and authority

Issues of space and ownership can be very sensitive. The new deputy will not necessarily be aware of all the background to such issues. In this incident, some typical areas for conflict are explored.

Part of the planning between the head and James, the new deputy, involved a discussion about improving communication with staff about significant pieces of information to do with school events, parents or students. They were concerned that there were some longer-term general pieces of information that all staff needed to know, and there were some urgent messages that needed to be delivered to staff on a daily basis. The school did not hold a daily staff briefing and to introduce one might – at this juncture – look like yet another pressure on staff time. Nor did the head and deputy consider it a good idea to send students round the school with messages, for security reasons (part of the site is detached from the main building). But some things needed to be communicated more urgently than at the weekly staff meeting.

So they decided on a scheme to use a part of an existing noticeboard in the staffroom as a vehicle for conveying messages. James took the initiative to make the board look as pleasant as possible. By backing it with coloured card and dividing it into labelled sections, it seemed to enhance the look of the room and to serve its intended purpose.

However, this simple act caused an immediate backlash. Nothing was said directly either to the head or to James, but it was obvious that a whispering campaign was afoot. Eventually they gleaned that some staff were unhappy about James's actions. The grounds of their complaints were apparently as follows:

- the staffroom is what it says, a room for staff, and should not be used for management purposes

- the noticeboard, though unused and sordid, was therefore the property of the staff and permission should have been sought before it was appropriated

- the deputy had no business to interfere with the staff's room or property in order to carry out the business of management, and should be reprimanded for his presumption.

The only way to deal with this situation was to challenge the troublemakers. So James asked them what their problem was. When they explained, he pointed out that no part of the school belonged exclusively to any one group of people: it was all there to further the education of students. The other options, such as coming to school earlier for a daily briefing, were spelled out. James suggested that if there were any similar incidents in the future they should speak openly and not gossip in corners.

TASK 9

Handling a delicate staffroom situation

Read over the case again and try to sort out the rights and wrongs of the situation. In particular, consider the perspectives of the three main parties to the incident:

- the head
- the deputy, James
- the disaffected staff.

Have you ever experienced a similar situation – either as a manager or as a participant? What happened? How did you feel?

The incident has been described here from James's point of view. Rewrite it from the perspective of the staff.

Finally, write a sequential list of the steps you would have taken if you had wanted to achieve better communication in the situation described here.

This is the moment to break off to consider some theoretical issues in relation to the topics of consultation, communication and conflict. The broader issues of leadership style are dealt with in Chapter 5.

Consultation

In one instance known to us, a newly appointed deputy was approached by one of the more assertive members of staff in a very public forum and asked:

> *'Will you negotiate with us about all the issues that arise during your appointment?'*

The deputy judged this to be a formative moment, and replied:

> *'No.' [Stunned silence.] 'I will consult whenever possible.'*

So what was the difference and why was it important? Recourse to the dictionary contains the answer.

> *Consult: Take counsel; seek information and advice; spend a period of reflection.*
>
> *Negotiate: Confer with another with a view to compromise.*

Both courses of action are possible as management options, but you have to decide which is likely to prove best for the situation and for the institution.

Task 10 may help you order your thoughts on the issues here.

TASK 10

Deciding between consultation and negotiation

Use the pro forma below to weigh the relative merits of consultation and negotiation as management ploys:

	Pros	**Cons**
Consultation		
Negotiation		

———— Communication ————

While managers may want to set the agenda about the tenor of communication between themselves and other members of staff, the importance of good-quality communication cannot be over-stressed. It is worth remembering the fundamental principle here:

> *Communication is a two-way process.*

Information giving, or the communication of decisions by the head, deputy or senior management team, is simply not enough; good management rests on the ability to give everyone a voice, even when it is clearly understood that the final decision has to remain with a member or members of management.

It is worth spending a little time now looking at some of the factors that make communication with staff more, or less, effective.

Communication is about how messages are sent (e.g. from members of the management team such as the deputy to workers, i.e. staff members). It is also about how the messages are received:

- whether they are understood (in clear language, properly explained)
- whether the intended audience is open to receiving them (whether their attitudes are positive or negative to the sender(s) or to the content of the message itself)
- whether the message is received (i.e. acted on, sabotaged or ignored).

In Table 4.1 we look at some of the factors that militate against effective communication.

TABLE 4.1 Barriers to effective communication

1 Failure to review, consult or listen (thus the message may be flawed, because it ignores key factors).

2 Failure to provide a context for the message (how and when a system will operate, and whether and what the exceptions are).

3 Failure to explain the purpose of the message (e.g. why a procedure is being changed or introduced).

4 Failure to persuade enough or key staff of the need for the message (thus the ground is not adequately prepared).

5 Failure to couch the issue in clear language (so it is not really intelligible or sufficiently clear).

6 Failure to explain the message clearly (in sequence, without omissions etc.).

7 Failure to time the message appropriately (e.g. delivering it just before a vacation, when people will forget it).

8 Failure to send the message to the correct people (perhaps informing co-ordinators or heads of department, but relying on them to relay it accurately to others).

9 Failure to deliver the message in the best format(s) (sending it by e-mail, when most people would have read the noticeboard sooner, or vice versa).

10 Failure to articulate the stake that each receiver has in the successful implementation of the message (because actions are best implemented when the doer has a stake in the outcome!).

In the same way, in some institutions a culture develops that receivers of management messages develop ploys to avoid receiving these messages. Here are just a few:

- I didn't see the notice

- I didn't think this applied to me/my year group/my class

- I misunderstood what you were saying

- I didn't have time – I was teaching

- I assumed it meant we were starting next term

- It won't work in my room because …

You can add some more from your own developing experience.

So if we want to make communication successful, what are the factors that help remove ambiguity and resistance, and help promote understanding and acceptance? At this stage in the book it may be opportune to deal with four significant factors:

- listening skills

- clarity of verbal expression

- understanding non-verbal communication

- understanding the communications network in the school.

However, before looking at these four factors in a little more detail, it may be valuable for you to begin to order your own thoughts on the topic of communication to date, and to do this through an activity – Task 11 – based on a case study of a real situation, recounted by one of our deputies.

CASE STUDY

Schools sports may not be sugar and spice!

Just after I was appointed I was informed that it was the deputy's role to organise the sports afternoon, which was a tradition in the school. A number of dignitaries, as well as parents, attended, so I felt it important that it should go well.

My first step was to ask my colleagues about the organisation of the day on previous occasions: who did what, what events were run, what prizes were offered, who sat where and so on. But this proved to be a thankless approach.

There was a great deal of information, but much of it was contradictory or ambiguous. It also contained a lot of historical detail about who would be offended if they were not asked to run a specific event. I felt that some of this information was probably true, but that some was deliberately designed to confuse or mislead. In short, one or two mischievous people were trying to stitch me up in this very public forum. Certainly, the students and the ancillaries I talked to produced conflicting accounts, for example, from those of some of the staff.

Before things got out of hand, therefore, I opted for a more formal approach, where I hoped this process would be more difficult – so I called a formal staff meeting. I invited also those ancillaries I felt would be likely to be involved. At this meeting I made staff articulate precisely what had happened in the past; and I asked for preferences from them about which events they prefer to be involved with. But I made it clear that, in order to organise the event well, I would have to have a final say.

Then I drew up a detailed written plan – including timetables, the layout of the sports field, and seating plans for guests. I added a list of individual responsibilities, with brief job descriptions. This was circulated to everyone.

The day itself dawned fine – thank goodness – and it all went reasonably well, too; so I felt I had not wasted my effort. Afterwards, one of the ancillaries came up and said: 'Well done! At least no one put one over on you.'

TASK 11

Analysing communication skills

Look back over the case study above.

What can you learn from it about communication between the deputy and the staff, ancillaries and students in this school?

What could have been done better?

Identify the key learning points that this case study contains about effective communication.

Now that you have undertaken Task 11, and have thought about communication with staff in a little more detail, it is time to revisit the four significant factors in communication.

Listening skills

Before management decisions are taken, it is useful to listen to what others have to say about the issue in hand. This listening can be of various kinds and involve a variety of target groups. Some ideas are detailed in Table 4.2.

TABLE 4.2 Dimensions of listening

1 Listening to whom?

- outside experts (consultants, LEA officers, inspectors, governors)

- SMT

- all teaching staff

- all staff, including non-teachers

- students

- parents/governors

- the wider community.

2 Listening to what?

- formal consultation

- at a staff meeting

- individually sought, considered opinions

- casual views and opinion

- gossip.

3 Listening in what context?

- in contrived surroundings (e.g. an appraisal interview)

- in rank-conscious exchanges (either side of a desk)

- in conversation (one professional to another)

- with a closed mind

- with an open mind

- privately or publicly.

4 Listening how effectively?

- With concentration

- Selectively.

The deputy has to remember the really important issue that relates to listening as a management skill:

Listening to the words is not the same as listening to the message.

Clarity of verbal expression

Having listened to advice, where appropriate, and mulled over what to do, the deputy has to translate the decision into a clear formulation of intent in order to communicate it to others. This part of the communication process requires from the deputy a high level of skill as an explainer. Effective explaining is dealt with in *Questioning and Explaining in Classrooms* (Kerry, 1998). It is not our intention to repeat the advice here except to reinforce that every effective explanation or instruction needs to pay attention to the following factors:

- clarity of purpose
- clarity of language
- definition of ambiguous terms
- correct sequencing
- completeness – lack of omissions
- concrete examples, where appropriate
- a clear summary.

These factors apply whether the instruction or decision is communicated orally, in writing, on a noticeboard, via e-mail or in any other medium.

Understanding non-verbal communication

While the good quality of oral explanation may assist in communication with staff, other factors also impinge on that process. One of the most important of these factors is non-verbal communication.

Non-verbal communication deals with the messages we send not with our words but with our bodies: a shrug, a smile, a sigh, a nod, a blink, a wink, a frown, a handshake.

Some people find their thoughts written transparently on their faces or in their body language. We have only to see such a person from a distance to know what mood they are in, for example. It is difficult for them to give a message orally without betraying their real thoughts. Such transparent people have to learn always to match their verbal and non-verbal communication, and they are best advised to stick to playing their lives in a very honest and straightforward fashion.

Others gravitate to the opposite extreme. We observe them, but find it almost impossible to know what they are thinking. They are inscrutable and are often viewed with suspicion by colleagues because they lack the usual clues about human interaction.

Most of us are neither so inscrutable nor so transparent. We need to learn to control our non-verbal communication so that we don't send messages that conflict with our words. If we produce frequent conflicts in our audience, then we lose the trust of those around us. The subtlety of body language is quite hard to master, but it operates at a subliminal level and is very important in our daily relations with people. A little time spent 'observing ourselves' (that is, making ourselves more conscious of the messages we are giving) can pay dividends in a management context.

A careful use of body language can be very useful in cementing a feeling of empathy between the deputy and the staff with whom he/she has to deal. The control of body language, combined with effective use of listening skills, can be powerful tools in managing our colleagues.

Understanding the communications network in the school

However well we relate to the people we manage, it is useful to have an understanding of the ways in which – in our specific institution – the communications network operates.

Take a very simple example from ordinary life. We sometimes hear people say something like this: 'I told Mavis (or Mervyn) in strict confidence. That way I knew everyone would find out in 24 hours without my having to tell them!'

The speaker understands that, in their circle of acquaintances, Mavis (or Mervyn) is the one who cannot keep a secret and who will operate the communications structure (probably the telephone) to pass on the gossip.

The same basic principle holds true in institutions such as schools. Each school develops both formal and informal communications structures. The informal ones are led by the staffroom Mavises and Mervyns. The formal ones are teams, departments, committees, working parties; they use discussion, oral briefings, papers, minutes, reports or e-mail through which to communicate.

It is useful for a new deputy to begin to map out the various formal and informal communications structures that operate in the school. Often it is helpful to use diagrams to do this (but remember to keep your jottings at home, and well away from those who might access your papers or your computer).

As soon as you begin to do this you will discover that some of these diagrams are more useful than others – that some structures work better. A few examples will suffice. Thus in Figs 4.1 and 4.2 we have two circular communication structures. In Fig. 4.1, communication exists between the centre (you as the deputy, for example) and each member of staff; but there is no communication between individual staff members. In Fig. 4.2, all staff (including you as deputy) are able to communicate on equal terms. By contrast, in Fig. 4.3 we see a very closed or hierarchical pattern of communication: a literal chain of command.

FIG. 4.1 The wheel of communications

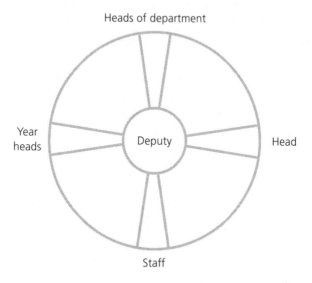

FIG. 4.2 The circle of communications

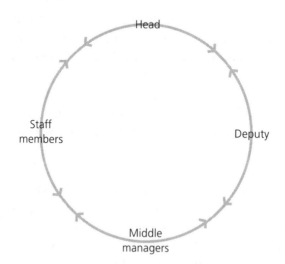

FIG. 4.3 The chain of communications

Head

Deputy

SMT

Heads of department

Year heads

Teachers

When you have given this issue of communications structures some thought, try Task 12.

TASK 12

Analysing the value of different communications structures

What communications structures exist in your school?

In each case, identify what is effective and what is ineffective about that structure.

Now work out some more effective structures that you might help to put in place.

What makes your preferred structures better?

How could you begin to implement them?

Conflict

However well we try to communicate with others, and however subtle the skills we apply to the business of communicating, conflict remains an inevitability for managers.

Not all conflict is bad: good-tempered conflict that generates sound debate and creative tension can be positively good.

Colleagues who appear mildly abrasive, who can always see the flaws in your suggestions and who think deeply can be mildly disturbing. But if they are also open to good ideas, able to mould their thinking to accommodate them and are prepared to be persuaded, then – properly handled – those colleagues can be outstanding assets. None of us has a total monopoly on either knowledge or wisdom, and people who improve and refine our ideas or spark us off to be (yet more) inventive are worth their weight in gold.

One of the best compliments we have heard paid to a deputy went like this:

> When you came I thought you would be like the others. But you were never afraid to listen to my ideas. I was grateful for that, and though we didn't always end up on the same side, I knew you respected my opinions and I respected yours. I've even changed some of my opinions!

But the fundamental conflict for the deputy is well summed up by one of our secondary colleagues:

> Teachers will always be looking to see how far you will go to support them. This support is in two basic directions. First, in the classroom or with parents when difficult situations arise. Second, with the head. But make no mistake about it. While you have to do the former to remain credible, as far as the management of the school goes, as a deputy you are no longer a member of staff, you are a manager. There can be no compromise about this.

For secondary deputies, and those in larger primary schools, who probably have a personal space or a shared senior management room into which to retreat, this may be fairly easy to handle. But for deputies in smaller primaries, who are still fundamentally teachers and who share the staffroom with other teaching colleagues and ancillaries, matters can be a bit more abrasive and difficult to cope with.

One of the key points that we have been at pains to point out in this chapter is that it is not realistic to assume that everyone you manage wants to be managed or is prepared to co-operate with your management decisions and actions. While in the last resort conflict has to be faced, one of the skills of the good manager is nevertheless the ability to avert it, avoid it, defuse it or use it to more productive ends. So it is on this more optimistic note that the chapter ends, by setting out in Table 4.3 some additional procedures to minimise conflict, whether this is between yourself and some members of staff or between two groups of third parties.

TABLE 4.3 Some procedures to minimise conflict and its effects

- listen to all the arguments
- list all the arguments – and their pros and cons
- learn to separate the rational from the emotional
- separate the issues from the personalities
- identify who will benefit from any given course of action
- avoid self-interest
- expose attempts by others to put self-interest before the good of the school
- develop the skill of tactfulness
- if appropriate, look for trade-offs
- prevent personal attacks by one faction on another
- seek to discover, and get others to articulate, their real motives for holding a specific view
- try to avoid 'militant' language
- don't allow verbal attacks on opponents
- make it clear that the end product of discussion cannot be just a 'fudge'
- draw out shared views and perceptions
- emphasise areas of agreement
- don't delay decisions – delay makes a situation fester, so keep to the agreed timetable
- concentrate on the goals rather than the means to achieve them
- use a skilled external agent to reflect back to protagonists the consequences of their positions.

Perhaps the best piece of advice of all, however, is one that features in Stephen Covey's seminal book, *The Seven Habits of Highly Effective People* (1992). This Covey calls 'Think Win/Win'. He claims it has five elements:

1. Identifying the desired results: what has to be done and by when.
2. Specifying the parameters: the policies and procedures within which the results have to be accomplished.
3. Identifying the resources: human and material, to achieve the results.

4 Setting up accountability: saying what standards have to be achieved, and the timescales for achievement.

5 Specifying the consequences of not achieving the results.

Without being too simplistic, we can paraphrase this approach as fixing the goals and spelling out the reality that not achieving them will be worse for everyone.

None of the approaches suggested here will work on every occasion; some are easier to pursue than others; the list is not exhaustive. But often you will find that diplomacy will win the day, and that your skills in situations involving conflict, or potential conflict, will grow and improve.

———— Summary ————

Our intention is that, at the end of this chapter, you will have:

- reflected on issues of relationships with other staff

- looked critically at means of effective communication in the school

- improved specific communication skills (listening, non-verbal skills)

- considered some ways in which to deal with conflict situations among staff.

The deputy as leader

This chapter has two broad purposes. The first is to examine the nature of leadership, comparing the concepts of leader and manager. The second is to invite you to look at the issue of leadership style, while providing you with opportunities to assess something of your own preferred style and how you come across to others.

———— Leader or manager? ————

This heading encapsulates what some construe as the horns of a crucial dilemma (which of these am I?), but what others regard as a pseudo question (deputies, heads and senior post holders in the public and private sectors generally have to be both, they would argue). Let us pursue the question analytically before making a decision.

Some educationists hold management, or education managers, in bad odour because – they feel – the concept of management derives from a commercial and industrial context (involving, for example, the manufacture of inert products, competition, advertising, profit etc.) that is wholly inappropriate to the teaching of students. Indeed, some of the developments in the 1980s, such as when colleges of further education were pressurised into trying to 'measure' their 'performance' in terms of British Standards drawn up for the manufacture of hard goods, seemed to vindicate this point of view.

But the situation is not that simple. If it implies anything, then effective management implies keeping things in good order: having plans, providing resources, carrying out the processes of the institution efficiently, clarifying procedures, and achieving the goals identified for both consumers and employees. In this context, one could see management as a laudable, but essentially mechanistic, process. In a schools context, the late 1980s were riddled with planning to these kinds of ends – school development plans, professional development plans, policy documents, even the National Curriculum. The 1990s were shot through with attempts to assess the success of such management plans: league tables, Ofsted inspections, and the rise of the Teacher Training Agency and other quangos to control curriculum or standards.

To parallel the rise in the popularity of management as a working concept in schools, there were attempts to improve the ability of managers. So we have seen a succession of 'management initiatives': the School Management Task Force, Headlamp courses, National Professional Qualification for Headship (NPQH) courses, and most recently a National College for School Leadership. None of these initiatives has *yet* yielded an outstanding set of successes in making schools better. So we have to ask: why not?

The plain truth is this: certain groups of teachers in schools (subject co-ordinators, heads of department/faculty, deputy heads and headteachers) do require management skills. But these skills cover a relatively limited spectrum of performance in the total fulfilment of these roles. What distinguishes good middle and senior managers from incompetent or average ones is a cluster of abilities that relate not to the skills of management alone, but to the process of leadership. It is to this distinction that we now turn our attention.

Leadership

In our view, education leadership is that part of the management process that provides progress towards new goals in a time of change. This progress can take place only through collaboration, teamwork and smooth organisation (sound management). Thus leadership is at the cutting edge of change, while management becomes part of the armoury of tools through which the change is achieved. Management and leadership are inter-related but distinguishable (*see* Fig. 5.1).

FIG. 5.1 The inter-relationship of management and leadership

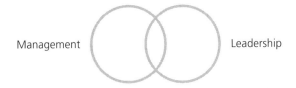

Let us explore the nature of school-based leadership in a little more detail. In a recent lecture (Kerry, 1999), it was argued that, given the changing nature of schools and schooling, education managers of the future would indeed have no

choice but to develop characteristics more commonly associated with business practice than with education.

They would not only have to be entrepreneurs, however, they would also need a more elusive characteristic: charisma. There is a shared cluster of characteristics of the charismatic leader. He or she:

- holds revolutionary, i.e. far-reaching, views about the need for change
- is driven by an inner compulsion
- has authority among a group of followers
- establishes an effective bond with the led
- puts forward a clear mission or a strong message
- works actively (with others) to achieve the mission or realise the message
- is difficult to deflect from the declared intention.

One of the problems that some people have in relating to this kind of model is that it has overtones of two – conflicting – zones of experience: the religious (for which the Christ figure and Muhammad may be exemplars), and the totalitarian (exemplified by a certain German corporal). Some writers have opted for the descriptor 'entrepreneur' rather than 'charismatic' and have transferred the metaphor to a business context. Among these are Inger Boyett and Don Finlay (1995), who studied an outstandingly successful school in Nottinghamshire from this perspective, and who reached interestingly similar conclusions to those described here. The headteacher of this exemplary school had achieved four things:

- a process of cultural change to develop new values and goals
- a process of revenue generation to facilitate the values and goals
- a marketing process to communicate the new image
- a decision-making process to encourage entrepreneurial behaviour throughout the institution.

Another writer on school management, Patrick Duigan (1996), has a different approach, avoiding either label and called 'authentic leadership'. Among the characteristics of this are:

- get real – discover your authentic self, who you are as a person and as a professional
- maintain a holy curiosity – authentic leaders are good learners
- notice the dying sparrow – in times of traumatic change, we are obliged as leaders to take care of and defend the wounded and the grieving

- massage your mistakes – the 'cult of perfection' is the curse of modern organisational life

- be alive to the passionate side of organisational life [which, I think, was not a prophetic reference to 1998 events in the US President's Oval Office, but rather a view that people can and should care about the jobs they do and the places they work for]

- frame the confusion – manage the double-headed arrow [or, as one principal I used to work for would put it: 'The level of professional maturity one has is measured by the degree of tension one can live with'].

These three approaches, while not identical, share some common characteristics that go beyond the 'play by the rule book', 'run a tight ship' mentality of so-called effective management. Others, too, have developed useful concepts in this regard, such as Stephen Covey's (1992) seven habits of highly effective people:

1 Be proactive.

2 Begin with the end in mind.

3 Put first things first.

4 Think win/win.

5 Seek first to understand, then be understood.

6 Synergise (i.e. seek creative co-operation).

7 Sharpen the saw (i.e. undertake self-renewal).

To this one might add Kerry's two principles for beginning managers:

1 Get into the right mindset – identify the priorities.

2 Be a fly on the wall, even your own wall – analyse processes and people.

Likewise, Brent Davies and Linda Ellison (1997) argue that management plans must be replaced by strategic intent: the vision of where the school is going, along with a flexible and responsive approach to taking it there. The senior managers of schools for the future will have to be leaders first as well as having a degree of managerial skill. Their work will be characterised by 'vision', and by the drive and ability to turn vision into reality. They will have to operate in a world that takes account of both macro- and micro-political realities. People skills will be paramount. These new teacher/leaders will need to understand the tensions inherent in satisfying the stakeholders. They will be 'quality driven', and we should not forget that – in education – the key to all quality is an understanding of effective learning and teaching.

So how do you shape up to this outline of the education leader? Task 13 gives you a chance to reflect on the answer to this question.

TASK 13

Reflecting on your skills as a leader

Below you will find a list of ten characteristics of leadership. You have to try to make an honest assessment of yourself against each characteristic. There are two parts to this self-assessment process.

First, rate yourself on the five-point scale for effectiveness (1 = very effective; 5 = ineffective). Second, try to find one example of your behaviour that exemplifies the score you have awarded yourself; the more recent the example the better.

Use the pro forma to help focus your thoughts.

Item	5 4 3 2 1	Example
1 Do you face problems and learn from them?		
2 Are you visible to others: do you keep a high profile?		
3 Do you communicate with others effectively?		
4 Do you stand by your beliefs/values?		
5 Have you empathy: do you listen effectively?		
6 Do you set an example?		
7 Are you confident?		
8 Are you professionally credible?		
9 Are you forward looking?		
10 Are you part of the team?		

_____ Some more characteristics of leadership _____

The would-be leader in school needs to possess, or acquire, the skills made explicit in Task 13. But there are other characteristics that are also important to leaders. Among the most significant of these is creativity. In the changing environment of the twenty-first century, schools need senior staff, such as deputies, who:

- can attract new 'clients' in a market economy

- use resources creatively

- solve problems imaginatively

- develop organisational structures that break traditional moulds

- are proactive and anticipatory

- behave intuitively

- change climates productively

- challenge the status quo.

The other essential insight into leadership is that there has to be something to lead. Leadership implies team working. This is dealt with in more detail later in the chapter, but for the moment it might be useful to summarise the importance of this initial section through a quotation:

> *Leaders articulate and define what has previously remained implicit or unsaid: then they invent images, metaphors and models that provide a focus for new attention. By doing so, they consolidate or challenge prevailing wisdom. In short, an essential factor in leadership is the capacity to influence and organise meaning for the members of the organisation ... Managers are people who do things right and leaders are people who do the right thing.*
>
> (Bennis and Nanus, 1985)

—— Leadership styles and organisational styles ——

Leaders are not like peas in a pod and any attempt to clone them is doomed to failure. Their very individuality is part of what gives them an 'edge' – although they may share clusters of broad characteristics of the kind already described. But leaders operate in contexts, and it is to these contexts that we now turn our attention.

The newly appointed deputy may not be instantly aware of the nuances of context that operate in an unfamiliar institution. But a very productive early exercise would be to try to make some assessment of the new institution with a view to assessing that climate. We ask you to do this through Task 14 later in the chapter. But meanwhile, you should familiarise yourself with the following taxonomy of organisational styles.

The bureaucratic school

Bureaucratic theory is associated with the work of sociologist Max Weber. It rests on the assumptions that human behaviour within organisations like schools is rational (which it may not be) that there are clear goals (when there may not be) and that authority from above is accepted (while in practice it is often questioned). In bureaucratic institutions the system is more important than the people who operate it.

A real example of a bureaucratic school was a large comprehensive in a seaside town. In the foyer was displayed a large triangular diagram showing the head at the pinnacle, and all the staff members (deputies, heads of department and year etc.) in layers below the head. Needless to say the newest NQTs were painfully aware of where they stood in the scheme of things! In line with the implications of the diagram, the head's office was beyond the secretary's room, which itself was secreted behind a sliding frosted-glass panel. Access to the head was almost unheard of, and only occurred when he issued the summons – not the other way around.

This model lacks flexibility and the creativity to deal with rapid change.

The political school

Political models of operation are about power. Schools that operate according to such models stress the wishes of special interest groups (such as subject co-ordinators or year heads) rather than the unity of the organisation. Political models make the assumption that the goals and mission of the organisation (i.e. the school) are ambiguous and contested. Conflict between rival groups is used as a means to decide and achieve goals – either by negotiation or by the victory of one side over another. Schools like this will have developed factions, will probably operate through committee structures, and there will be a good deal of behind-the-scenes horse-trading for support or votes.

In our experience no school ever claims to operate on a political model and yet, strangely, many do exhibit the behaviours described above.

The collegial school

This is the most frequently claimed model of school organisation. A collegial model requires that 'there exist in the school structures in which members have equal authority and participate in decisions which are binding on each of them'. The fundamental feature of this model is consensus. Values would be held in common. The head would be the first among equals. Decisions would be on a one-member one-vote basis. Senior staff might chair committees and working groups, but each person's opinion would be equally weighted.

In the real world, such altruistic approaches do not exist very often. Indeed, it would be hard to justify such a model – thoroughly pursued – when it is the head and the governing body, and not the individual and collective staff members, who are legally accountable for the performance of the school.

The ambiguous school

Institutions that operate on the ambiguity model are characterised by unclear or inconsistent goals, by staff who do not understand procedures, and by solutions to problems that are formulated on a trial-and-error basis. Sometimes factors like split sites tend to contribute to the generation of schools in this category. But it is the hand-to-mouth solutions to problems that are probably the most characteristic and most damaging features of this sort of organisation. Sometimes the phrase 'organised anarchies' is used to describe schools of this type.

Of course, the tendency to operate in this fashion may be imposed from outside – see the case study below. To resist ambiguity behaviour in these circumstances is extremely difficult.

CASE STUDY

An organised anarchy at work

A headteacher and a governor were sitting down together to fulfil a management task in a large suburban primary school: the task of operating the admission criteria in order to inform those parents whose children could be accommodated in the following academic year. The criteria were carefully drawn up and modelled on the LEA's guidelines. The pair worked diligently from 9.00 am and had just finished an intake list based on the criteria when … the courier from the LEA delivered the mail.

The mail contained a bombshell. The LEA had revised the number of admissions from 60 to 70! The decision was based on the floor space of the school, and that in turn had taken into account the opening of a newly built area that had been paid for with privately raised funds. Phone calls to the LEA confirmed that – though the intention of the benefactors had been to give the *existing* children more space – there was no discretion over the raised intake.

The head and the governor sat down and revised the intake list up to the new figure of 70 pupils. The school secretary mailed the acceptance notices to the appropriate parents.

The following day a letter arrived from the LEA. It revealed a further revised admission number – between the two previous figures.

(Adapted from *Primary School Manager*, May/June 1997, by permission of the editor and Pitman Publishing.)

What kind of organisation do you belong to?

This is a good moment for someone relatively new to the deputy's role to take stock of the institution you have joined. If you have not yet obtained a deputy post, then try to carry out the activity on your current school, or on one that you know well but can observe from a detached position. Use Task 14 to guide your investigation.

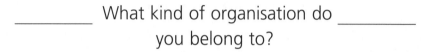

Assessing your organisation's style

Use the four models described above to analyse the style of working of your own chosen school. It is unlikely that your school will exhibit characteristics of just one style: most organisations contain a mixture of operational models. Examine the models and try to find examples of each one in the operation of your school.

Style   **Example**

The bureaucratic school

The political school

The collegiate school

The ambiguous school

What do the results of your survey tell you about the kind of leader you need to be? Can you formulate some early intentions for bringing about change?

Leadership style and the role of the deputy

The deputy head cannot set the whole tone and style of organisation for a school; the head plays a major role in determining this. But a sound partnership between the deputy and the head can have a significant influence on the relationships and methods of working that operate among the staff and that determine the ways in which decisions are taken and actions implemented. Above all, the mindset of the school, its openness to ideas and its creative ambience will be determined in part by the deputy. So your behaviour and example in this role are hugely important.

Task 13 earlier in this chapter started you off in thinking about your personal style and Task 14 asked you to assess the organisational style within which you work. Management theorists have construed the relationships between the leader and the organisation as a continuum, thus:

Results oriented _____ relationships oriented

Or again:

Concern for outcomes _____ concern for people

You might give some thought to where you might be, at this moment, on each of these continua – and also to where you might like to be in a year or two.

In general, as a newcomer to the business of leadership you will probably tend to start closer to the results/production end of the continuum. You may feel you need to establish your authority, to be seen to get results, to establish your right to make decisions. A common manifestation of this – and we have all been there in the early days of authority – is what might be termed 'management by memo'. We make isolated decisions, send messages, expect change, impose accountability on others for the decisions we have taken.

Experience moves us further to the right of the continuum. We recognise the need to get others to own decisions, and at least to appear to take them for themselves. We come to agreements rather than resort to directives. We ask colleagues to be accountable in the first instance to themselves for their performance, and to seek support if they have problems. Authority figures who fail to make this 'journey to the right' often develop into resented demagogues.

But a step too far to the right-hand end of the continuum moves us dangerously close to resigning personal responsibility for the decisions we are paid to take. It suggests that authority no longer rests with us, and that colleagues are no longer accountable at all. If the continuum is a tightrope, success is staying balanced and upright somewhere out in the middle of it.

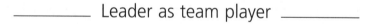

Leader as team player

There is an inherent problem with leadership – or at least with the versions of leadership that we earlier labelled charismatic. Highly creative people may not translate easily into team players. This dilemma is dealt with here.

It may seem contrary to advocate that deputies need to be entrepreneurs and charismatics, and also to describe them as team players. The truth, as often, is stranger than the myth: you can be both. The trick is that it takes a degree of understanding about how teams work and a good deal of self-discipline.

We find the key in the writings of Meredith Belbin (1993). Belbin argues that in order to achieve a task effectively you need a range of skills. But few of us have all the skills in full measure. Properly constructed, a team can incorporate people who do cover the range of skills required for the task. The downside is that each will also have some shortcomings, but these Belbin regards as 'allowable weaknesses' provided that they do not inhibit the working of the team.

For example, if we want to drive forward a curriculum innovation, the team would need someone with vision to formulate the big picture about what needed to be achieved. It would also need someone to co-ordinate the actions of the team members. Some of the work might be quite detailed timetable experimentation. New resources might be required. So a team of four people with these specific skills might work better than an individual who was stronger on some areas than others: good at vision, poor at implementation; or a nitpicking timetabler but unimaginative at obtaining resources.

Belbin identified a number of team roles that could be played in most teams to drive an initiative forward. These were:

- the co-ordinator, who controls the work of the team. He or she will have positive qualities of enthusiasm, assertiveness and a sense of duty; but the same person may be quite weak at being creative or inspirational;

- the implementor, who translates ideas into practice and can work with attention to detail; an organised, self-disciplined individual;

- the shaper, who inspires others and pushes them hard to get things done. His or her allowable weakness may be impatience!;

- the innovator, who advances new ideas and may be very creative and intelligent, but who may not be a 'people person';

- the resource investigator, who works well with people and can ferret out resources from within and outside the team; who may be sociable but may become bored without a challenge;

- the monitor/evaluator, who is a systematic thinker and sifter of problems, but who may be rather negative and pessimistic – the one who would always see a half empty cup rather than a half full one;

- the completer/finisher, who is obsessed with deadlines;

- the team worker, a social extrovert who may have to be kept on task by others; the one who does the legwork of the team;

- the specialist, who has important skills, but may not share the overall vision of the team.

Since not all teams are large enough to cover the nine roles set out above with separate individuals, team members often have to play more than one role. Most of us do, in practice, have skills in more than one area, but many people have areas where their functioning is quite ineffectual.

So the deputy as a team player has to have an eye to both constructing and leading teams. If we want to run our schools in a way that is participative (if not literally 'collegiate', *see* above) then we need to give tasks to teams. These teams may be committees, but are more likely to be working groups who are commissioned to undertake activities on behalf of the whole school. In building a team, the deputy has to take into account the strengths and weaknesses of the members. But often the deputy is a team member, so it is important for you to know and understand your own team role: what you are good at, and what you need others to do for you.

Task 15 asks you to think about your strengths in the context of team membership and team leadership.

TASK 15

Being a team member and team leader

Look at Belbin's nine team roles again, as set out below. Using the list as a prompt, and referring back to the text in this section, try to assess your strengths and weaknesses as a team member.

Role	My strengths	My weaknesses
Co-ordinator		
Implementor		
Shaper		
Innovator		
Resource investigator		
Monitor/evaluator		
Completer/finisher		
Team worker		
Specialist		

When you have compiled your self-analysis, think about your weaknesses. In a team that you put together, are there one or two team roles that would normally have to be played by people other than yourself? What are these?

Now try to watch a team at work, in school or outside it – preferably one in which you play a minor role – and use the nine categories to analyse what is happening during team sessions. Can you see the system at work?

In team working and team leading there are three main principles to which you have to adhere:

- the task must be achieved
- the team must be built up and maintained
- individuals within the team must be developed to fulfil their potential.

To comply with these principles you cannot have a 'woolly' or comfortable view of team working that is driven merely by ideals of cosiness and togetherness. Even in a small primary school, it is a total myth that any contentious issue can be resolved by making a cup of tea and sitting round the staffroom table for a friendly chat about it. There are always a few people whose adopted role in life is to sabotage any progress or denigrate any idea, so consensus as such is not an option.

However, when problems are dealt with by teams, and when team working operates effectively, this method can have real advantages. It generates ownership and improved morale. It has considerable potential for shared wisdom. It probably lowers stress and improves accountability. It achieves a degree of delegation without loss of overall control. Team working and team leading are important management tools, and must be developed by deputies in order to promote their roles.

—————— Why teams fail ——————

Finally in this chapter, it may be opportune to look very briefly at why teams sometimes fail. If teams form a significant platform in the deputy's leadership style they have to succeed. Understanding the causes of failure may help to eliminate it.

Teams often fail because of the way their meetings and agendas are organised. They become too much like committees and not enough like working groups. The emphasis shifts from process and action to procedure and debate. This in turn leads to a tendency for teams to become reactive rather than proactive. The roles of the shaper and the innovator are crucial here. It is interesting that, in such team or group situations, the person who offers ideas is often regarded as something of a maverick, an 'odd-ball' who disturbs the smooth working of the team, when he or she should be valued as an asset.

Teams often grind to a halt because they do not put enough energy into personal renewal, into gaining new experience and ideas, and into developing their members professionally and personally. A team is only as good as the collective abilities of the members who comprise it.

Many of these themes will be revisited in later chapters.

—————— Summary ——————

So far in this book we have examined five relatively broad themes to do with the job of the deputy and with becoming and being a deputy. We have looked at the early experiences of deputies new in the job, at relationships with the head, at the variety of roles that deputies are called on to play, at establishing staffroom relationships and at developing styles of leadership.

The remainder of the book tends to focus on rather narrower themes. It may be helpful for you to think of the first five chapters as defining the context of being a deputy, and the rest of the manual as a collection of chapters that will assist you in developing individual skills that will help you perform more effectively.

Our intention is that, at the end of this chapter, you will have:

- explored more deeply the contrasts between leadership and management in schools
- made links between leadership/management theories and your own school situation
- examined the value of teams and team working.

Managing time

The most surprising thing about books purporting to help school-based managers and leaders is that very few of them contain a chapter about managing time. Of all the individual skills that a manager, at any level and in any business, can learn, the effective management of time is probably one of the most important.

——— Problems of time ———

At the risk of offending some readers, it is important to say at the outset of this chapter that teacher-managers are some of the very worst managers of time in the world of management. But why do we say this?

Schools are full of human beings – students, teaching colleagues, non-teaching staff – any of whom is likely to make demands at any moment. Teachers generally (and, of course, there are exceptions) have learned to deal with this by responding instantly to these demands for immediate attention (i.e. they have become reactive), leaving less demanding tasks (mail, planning, preparation) to more private moments. Proactivity often flies out of the window. Teachers are classic examples of failure to comply with the old management adage:

> *Distinguish the important from the urgent.*

Anything that claims urgency and immediateness gains over things that are crucial but not pressing. 'Miss, I need a new book' takes precedence over 'Miss Smith, please can you redevelop this portion of the science curriculum'. Of course, there are reasons for this; but for a deputy the reactive mode of management can only spell disaster. What this chapter argues is that the balance has to be intelligently redressed.

Similarly, teachers have mental time maps that are firmly rooted in the term structure. English education is almost inexorably embedded in a three-term agricultural calendar. This is not the place to argue the case for more intelligent use of school time through calendar reform, only to note one of the effects of *not* doing this. In any circumstance where a school has to carry out a piece of reform, make a decision, even reply to a request, the answer will almost certainly be along the lines of 'after half-term', 'next term', 'next academic year'. These timescales for operation are simply too long-winded for effective management in a time of rapid change in education. The phrases become excuses for inertia rather than deadlines for action.

In this chapter we attempt to identify some of the conflicts facing teacher-managers and to offer some advice about ways in which the deputy head can take greater control of managing time.

Distinguishing the important from the urgent

In the previous section we recalled the management adage about the need to distinguish the important from the urgent, and this may be a good place to begin thinking about time-management skills.

One of the certainties of life as a deputy is that, once established in the role, tasks will come at you thick and fast. Distinguishing importance from urgency must become a kind of permanently embedded filing system in your brain by which you decide which jobs to do in what order. You could construe it something like Fig. 6.1.

FIG. 6.1 Deciding on important and urgent tasks

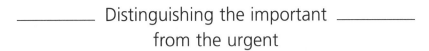

Important and urgent	Urgent
Important	Neither urgent nor important

Before the start of each day, invest a few minutes deciding which tasks for the day belong in each of the boxes. What results is a priority list for action. Tasks that are important *and* urgent receive immediate attention. Important jobs take second place, but also receive attention. Urgent jobs get done, but are kept in perspective so that they do not dominate in importance or order. Tasks that are neither important nor urgent take the lowest priority.

This construction of priorities always receives some surprised looks from trainee managers, and often some objections, of which the following are typical.

Objection: If a job is urgent, how can I ignore it?

The system does not say ignore it, it says get it in perspective. How urgent is it? To whom? Often, so-called urgent tasks can be done within their own timescales provided the rest of the manager's life is properly organised; in other words, provided the important jobs are done first. If a child comes to you bleeding profusely, then the situation *is* urgent and calls for instant action. But let's say that you receive a questionnaire from your local teacher training institution about how they can improve their service to you. It has a deadline date for three days' time. Is it urgent? Is it important? You may decide that it is not among the most important jobs you have to do, but it may be something you feel is in your and the school's overall interest to do. In importance, this task is not a high priority. Is it urgent? It has a deadline, but it is not your deadline. It may be inconvenient for the institution to receive it a day or two late, but that may be better than not receiving it. On the other hand, it will take a day in the post; but if you fax the response you can gain a day in which to give it attention. The job can probably be done, but not *now* as it appears to demand. You can manage it, within the deadline, maybe by using marginal time (*see* below).

Objection: What do I do with non-important, non-urgent jobs?

You may decide to do them. This will depend on many factors:

- how much pressure you are under
- how much you want to please the person who asked you
- whether you think there is any value in doing the task, and so on.

But, *you may decide not to do them*. This often sounds like heresy when the idea is first presented. You have to establish clear guidelines for what are and what are not useful and appropriate things for you to do. This may mean turning jobs away. The tradition that we all do any and every job presented to us from whatever source simply has to be questioned at times. You will decide that some jobs don't get done, or don't get done by you. Oddly enough, this rarely leads to controversy or complications!

In the light of what has been said in this section, now look at Task 16, which asks you to examine your own ways of prioritising and tackling jobs.

TASK 16

Prioritising and tackling jobs

Look back over all the jobs you have done as a deputy in the last week. Make a complete list.

Now examine the order in which you did them and how you prioritised them. What criteria did you use?

Use the box in Fig. 6.1 to reprocess and prioritise these jobs.

When you have done this, compare your two sets of priorities. What has changed? Why?

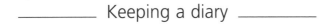

Keeping a diary

A few paragraphs ago we suggested that you sit down at the beginning of each day and plan the jobs for the day and their order of priority. Good managers keep diaries and lists. Of course, there are some commercial enterprises that make a lot of money from supplying 'system stationery' for such purposes, but you don't need to spend your own or the school's money on these unless for personal image creation. A basic kit for efficient operation is a diary laid out so you can view a week at a time, probably A5 in size (big enough to write in, small enough to carry about), and some small cards or memo sheets on which to make your daily lists. The procedure is also simple enough:

- before work, check the diary for fixed points (lessons, meetings, visitors);
- prioritise the jobs for the day and make a list;
- during the day update your list (cross off completed tasks, add essential new ones, reorder the priorities);
- at the end of the day recheck the diary;
- start tomorrow's list of priorities.

There is no mystique about being organised: it is an attitude of mind. But to stay organised you have to be disciplined. Here are some hints that may help:

- when you organise meetings, set a beginning *and* an end time (*see* Chapter 12);

- when you fix interviews with individuals, make sure you allow enough time for the likely discussion, but then stick firmly to that time. You may have to signal the end of the interview politely ('I'm sorry, I have another appointment now');

- if you finish a task early or an appointment falls through, don't fritter away the opportunity: revert to the next priority on the list that you can do;

- build into your priorities on-going tasks such as lesson preparation; it takes time so you have to plan it in to your life;

- don't run late. It is bad manners, and the later you start the worse it will get. Insist on punctuality in others;

- don't book commitments when you should be pursuing other priorities such as being on the corridors or checking behaviour in the dining area.

Using a filing system

One of the features of a busy professional life is that you will need to retain a lot of information. Many managers make the error of trying to keep all this in their heads. It is more efficient to make records of crucial information such as the outcomes of meetings, decisions, policies and so on. Often it is useful to have rough notes about meetings with individuals or groups. All this builds into a huge amount of data.

Again, you can buy system stationery to cope with this, but generally it is simpler and cheaper either to keep paper records in a filing cabinet or to store your information in a personal computer. (Remember, though, that the cabinet should be locked if it contains personal information and you must comply with the requirements of the Data Protection Act if you use a database.) Your diary and priority lists can also now be stored on a micro-computer, but before you make the decision about which method to use, think about which will work best for you. The crucial advice is not to rely on your memory.

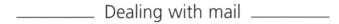

Dealing with mail

One of the worst management features of schools is that they fail to deal with mail effectively. As a deputy you will probably receive quite a lot of mail, and this may come as something of a shock to you at first. Opening and dealing with 20 letters a day can be daunting if you are not used to it. But this, too, can be made more efficient with some simple systems. Again, this is a task best done on a regular basis; probably at the end of school rather than the beginning, since the post may not have arrived beforehand.

The key with mail is to have a system:

- some will be delegated to others (e.g. heads of department)
- some will be filed without immediate action (e.g. catalogues relating to your subject teaching)
- some will need an answer and will become an item on your priority list
- some will be irrelevant and can be binned.

What you should not do is what was described to us by one individual:

> *I save all the mail. Each day I put it in a big cardboard box. I don't open it, unless it looks particularly important. Then, at the end of term, I go through it. If it's out of date I throw it away. If there are reminders to deal with it, for example by phone from the LEA, then I look for the item and deal with it.*

Yes, this was a real conversation – with the head of a primary school.

TASK 17

Sorting the mail

Keep a note of all the mail you receive for a fortnight.

Sort each piece using the headings below (or others you may care to substitute or add):

- delegated
- filed
- actioned/answered
- binned.

What proportion of this mail required action? What proportion could be disposed of instantly?

If you have e-mail, carry out a similar exercise with this. How do the results compare? (Sadly, e-mail seems to have vastly increased the number of messages that we have to read, but that require very little attention, even awareness.)

The items of mail, or e-mail, that reach your priority list as important/urgent need attention. The choices are:

- to respond by phone, fax or e-mail – which may be quicker than writing; but always keep a note of your reply in some form;

- to respond by letter – which may involve using a PC to generate your response yourself, or providing a response to a secretary on tape, in longhand or by dictation.

Whichever means you use, always check the end product yourself. Too many letters from schools to parents and official bodies go out with horrendous errors of grammar and spelling. These give an impression of shoddiness, at best.

———— Using marginal time ————

Time is a precious commodity and 'buying time' is an important skill. We have always found that using marginal time effectively can save hours of work.

Many of the jobs that a deputy has to do require some form of thinking and planning: curriculum innovation, setting up a new committee, working out the next week's assembly. Progress in many of these tasks can be made away from the workplace, and often in time that would be used for other, less cerebral activities. By making the most of this kind of marginal time you really can do two jobs at once.

Here are just a few examples of time we all have that could increase our work output for little real expenditure of time:

- while carrying out garden chores or DIY jobs;

- while doing mindless household chores;

- on trains or buses or while waiting their arrival;

- in the dentist's waiting room;

- queuing at the supermarket checkout;

- waiting in the car to pick up the children from football practice or dance class.

Planning and thinking can be carried out in these circumstances, perhaps reinforced at the end with some scribbled notes for use later back in the workplace when we come to finalise the job. The point of employing this marginal time in this way is not necessarily to provide employers with a free source of unpaid labour, it is to help us complete our work at the same time as saving real time for our own refreshment and relaxation: quality time.

———— Summary ————

Our intention is that, at the end of this chapter, you will have:

- started to analyse jobs into categories of importance and urgency
- considered the balance of time allocated to individual tasks within your own role
- reviewed your time management systems to check their efficiency
- understood the value of marginal time.

chapter seven

Learning, teaching and curriculum responsibilities

This chapter deals with one of the most critical areas of responsibility that can be afforded a deputy head. It is also one of the most daunting. The inevitable question is: how can I be an expert in all these things?

That deputies feel such insecurities is evidenced in some comments made to us by deputy heads:

> One interesting thing that I have found out through a recent appraisal is that, although I am someone who has an eye to a long-term future as a head, and while management skills are therefore very high on my personal agenda, the management element of my performance as a deputy is not critically challenged by teacher colleagues. They judge much more on classroom and overall teaching performance. It is the way I handle assembly or school productions that counts with them – the public face of the school. But I know I have not maintained my classroom as well as I might since I have been a deputy: it's a question of time and priorities. Teacher colleagues are fairly easily impressed about my skill as a manager – though I know I have a lot to learn. But they are unforgiving about anything that has to do with teaching.

Another deputy reported:

> On being newly appointed as a deputy, and meeting my class for the first time, I had several agendas. To the class I wanted to indicate my expectations about behaviour, that I wasn't a 'soft touch'. But I also wanted to put across planned, stimulating and challenging lessons. I needed to show other colleagues that I could teach at least as well as them, and I was conscious of their taking soundings about me.

These two deputies had to lead curriculum development across the subject spectrum, and clearly were expected to outperform the teachers at the core business of teaching.

In this chapter it is our intention to try to disentangle precisely what skills a good deputy needs to fulfil the expectations of staff and the head in the areas of learning, teaching and curriculum leadership. We then go on to explore how these areas come together in the business of continuing professional development – another area commonly led by the deputy head.

Learning

Schools are about learning. They are not about teaching, though teaching may (or sometimes may not) encourage and promote learning. Fundamentally, students attend school to learn – the formal curriculum, the informal curriculum, and the hidden curriculum. In an age of increasing public and political awareness of educational issues, this learning is measured, calculated, compared, contrasted, and forms the basis of accountability.

The deputy may not have ultimate responsibility for this aspect of the school's performance but will share tasks with the head. The deputy will need to be familiar with all the requirements of the National Curriculum, with other statutory requirements, with baseline testing procedures, with other statutory tests or public examinations, with arrangements for special needs provision, and with the publication of school performance data.

TASK 18

Familiarising yourself with the quality of learning in your school

What precisely is your school's achievement in terms of student learning?

Survey the performance of students in statutory/public assessments.

How does this compare with your baseline assessments?

What 'value' has the school 'added' for these students?

What problems or shortcomings are revealed by your survey?

What do you plan to do about them?

While these areas of knowledge about the performance of the school and its students form the backdrop to the process of monitoring learning, they are not in themselves the process. A deputy might, typically, be given the role of:

Fostering motivation, high self-esteem and independent learning.

This role – taken from an actual job description – captures the essence of the learning process. It is about style and ethos, not just about league tables of performance.

In one secondary school the performance of students began to drop dramatically. The deputy became very worried by this trend and called in an outside consultant. The consultant spent some time in the school analysing the issues. This is part of the report:

> *I found students who were more than averagely interested in their school work, and more than averagely motivated to do well. But these same students were less than averagely excited by school, and less than averagely able to concentrate on their work. Evidence for these statements was culled from two sources. First, I asked a random sample of students some quite detailed questions, and these were the conclusions I drew. Then I did some systematic observation in lessons. Students – or at least quite a lot of students – came prepared to lessons, and settled down to work with compliance and a degree of interest. But as lessons progressed a noisy minority gradually took over. Noise spilled into disruption. Over and over again this happened. In one lesson – quite a good lesson – the teacher ended up talking to empty desks while the students hung out of the classroom windows watching a police helicopter on manoeuvres. I concluded that motivation was relatively high, but that the conditions for exploiting this motivation were very low. The solution lies in three issues. First, establishing and maintaining clear standards of discipline. Second, in well organised, planned and interesting lessons. Third, in articulating and sharing the goals of learning between students and teachers.*

This report demonstrates that students in the school were motivated, but that the staff were not capitalising on this. The result was that students' self-esteem was falling. The students were not encouraged to be independent in their learning; but, worse, they were dependent on teachers who failed to capture their interest. In Task 19 you are asked to try to engage in some solutions to this problem.

TASK 19

Improving learning and attitudes to learning

What would you include in a learning policy for your school?

How would you set about implementing such a policy?

What would the role in implementation be of each of the following:

- the head
- the deputy
- heads of department/subject co-ordinators
- governors
- teachers
- non-teaching support staff
- parents?

One of the harder issues to deal with is independence in learning. Students learn better when they themselves are made responsible for the learning they undertake. It has become fashionable (at least in some political circles) to advocate the use of whole-class didactic teaching as a means of improving learning. There really is little, if any, evidence of the overall efficacy of this as a method of learning. It can provide an efficient short-term method of teaching in some limited circumstances (for example, where a body of information needs to be got across to a relatively homogeneous group of students). But as a learning method for repeated use it rates as the last resort of the creatively barren teacher.

Indeed, one could argue that, even for efficiency, whole-class teaching is less than the optimum option. A computer program would probably be as effective, and the students would probably like the work more. (In recent surveys students indicated that computer-based learning was almost universally regarded as a favourite method.)

Learning should embrace subtler factors. There needs to be a culture in the school that values learning. The achievements of students in intellectual activities have to be celebrated as much as their achievements in other fields, such as sport. The insults thrown at high-performing or low-performing youngsters have to be eliminated. Teachers might consider methods that give students pride in their work. Learning can be constructed so that it is subject to a variety of methodologies. Some students prefer listening, others active participation, or role play, or writing, or modelling – no one method can dominate to the exclusion of others. Preferred learning styles for students are as much as an issue as preferred teaching styles by staff. Success in learning is an important factor in students' self-esteem. Responsibility is another factor: knowing when work is due, keeping to deadlines, doing one's best.

The deputy may play a significant part in propagating these ideas and creating a sound psychological climate for learning: a learning ethos. In so doing the deputy will become, in a very real sense, the 'lead teacher', and colleagues are right to watch whether an example is set in the deputy's own classroom.

Teaching

As well as being a leader by example, a deputy may well play a role in monitoring the work of other teachers. He or she may become a key person in the quality assurance mechanism whereby the school checks that staff are doing a good and consistent job. The same kind of role may well embrace the supervision of any newly qualified staff, or those in training for the profession. Most deputies find this role rewarding because it makes them think more deeply about the fundamental role of the teacher; but many also have little experience in judging the work of others and are rather daunted by it.

A number of factors can greatly increase the deputy's skills as a person charged with maintaining standards of teaching. The key issue is that no deputy or head can have any systematic idea of what teaching is like in the school unless they take time out to observe some! Of course, walking round corridors, watching colleagues in informal situations, looking at the results their students achieve, and even peering through the glass doors of classrooms during lesson times will all provide data of more or less value. But only observing teaching in operation will provide valid evidence of classroom performance.

Those new to classroom observation are often diffident about the process. This is understandable, but it is possible to gain in confidence and competence. The process is more subtle than this, but there are three indispensable rules for observing a colleague:

- agree beforehand when the observation is to take place and what the focus of the observation is to be. It is not professional to say: 'I'll be in to see you some time next week. Just do what you normally do';

- use an observation pro forma on which to collect your observations, so that you have a record and an *aide memoire* of what you have seen;

- make an opportunity to feed back your thoughts as soon as possible after the lesson. Delay causes stress to the person being observed.

Having adopted the correct basic procedures, what are the purposes of observing colleagues and how can observation be carried out to achieve these purposes?

Observation can have a number of purposes, singly or in combination, for example:

- to act as a quality control mechanism within the school;

- to provide feedback to the teacher on performance;

- to give professional support or advice;

- to help the observer gauge the experience of students as consumers of lessons;
- to help the person observed concentrate on or develop a specific area of skill;
- to monitor an experimental piece of teaching or curriculum.

You may wish to devise specially constructed pro formas for particular observations. But here we offer just two examples, one for general use and one as a model for the observation of a specific skill. These are shown as Tables 7.1 and 7.2 (overleaf). When you have looked at these pro formas, and bearing in mind the advice in this section, you might like to try out one of the pro formas by observing a colleague at work, using Task 20.

TASK 20

Observing teaching

Select an occasion when you have to carry out an observation of teaching as part of your role as deputy. (If no opportunity is likely to occur, you might like to negotiate to watch a friend or colleague in another school – you may even invite this colleague to carry out the exercise on you, too!)

Agree with the person to be observed the groundrules for the observation (*see* above).

Now observe the lesson using either one of the pro formas suggested here, or one you have compiled yourself.

Feed back to the colleague after the lesson.

What did you learn from this process? In particular: what was easy, what was difficult, what would you do differently next time?

Very often there is little culture of lesson observation in schools. In these cases, an impending Ofsted inspection, or a follow-up to one, may provide the opportunity to carry out this kind of activity. But even without such an incentive, there is no need to be apologetic for monitoring teaching: it is a major purpose of schools to provide effective teaching, and a major task of management to ensure that teaching is effective. Of course, if you are a new deputy, observation should not be carried out without the agreement of the head, and not unless there is an open policy in the school about how and when teaching is to be monitored. Such monitoring may link to appraisal or a mentoring scheme, issues dealt with in more detail in Chapter 11.

TABLE 7.1 Pro forma for general lesson observation

Teacher observed:	**Date:**	**Time:**
Subject of the lesson:	**Student group:**	

The lesson intentions:
(These may be supplied in the teacher's lesson notes; otherwise you may try to deduce them)

Quality of preparation:

Learning and teaching method(s) used:
(Comment on appropriateness of student grouping – whole class, individualised learning etc. – on teaching skills such as discussion, questioning, use of audiovisual aids, quality of explanations, differentiation)

Class management and control:
(Discipline, behaviour of students, noise levels, transitions from one activity to another, entry and departure of students, application of students to tasks set)

Evidence of student learning:
(Examples of oral or written contributions to the lesson)

Lesson outcomes:
(What did the lesson achieve? Did this match with the intentions?)

Evaluation by the teacher:
(Did the teacher use feedback from students to amend the lesson as it progressed?)

Strengths and weaknesses of the lesson:

Other issues for discussion:

TABLE 7.2 Pro forma for observing a specific teaching skill

Teacher observed: **Date:**   **Time:**

Subject of the lesson: **Student group:**

Focus of the observation:

(*In this example, students' application to their tasks*)

How readily do students begin work when required to do so?
(Observe lesson beginning, and transitions in particular)

How effective is their concentration?

A dipstick measurement of time on task by students:
(To carry out this measure, watch each student for 60 seconds, recording the number of seconds during which he/she is engaged on the task. Record this in column A. Then watch the next student until each class member has been observed. The time on task of the class is the total number of seconds worked by all the students (= n) as a percentage of $60n$.)

	A Time working	B
Student 1:	secs	out of 60 seconds
Student 2:	secs	out of 60 seconds
Student n:	secs … etc.	

(Total time on task, all students (i.e. total of all scores in column A) over total seconds in column B [no. of students x 60], expressed as a percentage.)

What distracts students?

How does the teacher deal with distractions?

What are the issues about students' application to task that emerge from the observations:

Monitoring the quality of teaching will provide a great deal of information about the school, as well as about individual teachers. The head and the deputy together have to understand the need for confidentiality. But observing teaching will inevitably shed light on a lot of management data, for example:

- the strengths and weaknesses of the school
- the relative merits of different phases within the school
- the strengths of specific subject areas
- in-service training needs.

Curriculum issues

In the previous sections we have looked at some ways in which a deputy head can begin to make a difference to the quality of teaching and learning in the school. Other quality issues are dealt with in Chapter 9. Here we move on to examine the role of the deputy in managing an effective curriculum for the school, one of the commonest aspects of the role and one that appears in most job descriptions for deputy headship.

There is no easy way to say this: the key to success here is knowledge, and the only way to gain that knowledge is to spend a period of quiet study devoted to gaining it. Before you can tackle curriculum matters effectively, you will need to carry out the activities in Task 21.

TASK 21

Familiarising yourself with the whole curriculum

To be a good controller of curriculum issues you will need three kinds of knowledge:

1 Knowledge of the National Curriculum requirements for the phases of education represented in your school, and across all of the subjects taught.

2 Knowledge of the content of the curriculum that is taught in the discretionary time allowed, not covered by the National Curriculum.

3 Knowledge of the 'hidden curriculum' of the school – the intentions of the school with respect to ethos and attitudes.

Make an opportunity to provide yourself with a good working knowledge of these three areas. (You do not have to be a subject expert in every curriculum area to understand the main intentions and content that the National Curriculum requires to be delivered.)

Issues of assessment are dealt with in Chapter 9. Here, we shall look at the deputy's tasks that relate directly to ensuring that the planned curriculum of the school is delivered, rather than measuring the effectiveness of that delivery.

What does a deputy need to do in order to monitor the delivery of the curriculum?

In general terms, we have indicated that acquiring knowledge is a prerequisite; indeed, in an ideal world each deputy should also have at least an overview of the National Curriculum in the phases of education not covered by their own school. But the deputy cannot stop there. It is essential for the curriculum deputy to remain in tune with, and even at the cutting edge of, trends in how the curriculum is developing nationally (one might argue, internationally). Over recent years, for example, it would have been a poor deputy who did not grasp the importance of information and communications technology (ICT) to the developing school curriculum. To stay on top of the job the deputy must read the education press, attend conferences, talk widely to professional colleagues and so on. Continual updating is the key to effective curriculum leadership.

Of course, heads of subject departments and subject co-ordinators – if they are doing their jobs well – will be an invaluable source of information. Regular meetings with them to discuss trends may be advantageous. Don't rely on informal staffroom chat as a method. Hold brief meetings and keep notes of them.

Look at the school's policies for each curriculum area. Make sure that there is a mechanism for reviewing each policy on a regular basis. Review is more than endorsing its continuation: it is a rigorous process of improvement. It is helpful if each subject leader has to present and justify the policy of their area to the governors on a regular basis, say once a year, or every 18 months at most.

Policies contain intentions for the curriculum area. How can you be sure that these are being delivered? It is helpful to require subject leaders to establish meaningful criteria against which delivery can be measured. They can then be asked to provide data to support the view that the intentions really are being achieved. This data is most effective when it contains some assessment of student perceptions.

As deputy you can facilitate curriculum effectiveness by helping to find resources. This issue is dealt with in more detail in Chapter 14, Budgets and Finance. Here it is necessary only to say that the deputy must be creative in trying to deliver resources where they are needed, but also in monitoring the way resources that have been provided have been used. In one case we discovered, the deputy was pressurised very strongly by a subject leader for more resources for basic equipment. This deputy was certain that the money for these resources had been allocated. He checked the records, and indeed it had. He therefore challenged the subject leader as to why a second tranche of money was needed for something which had already been provided. On detailed investigation it emerged that the original order for the goods had been delivered, but to the second site of this split site school. What was lacking was not the resource but a proper monitoring procedure for the receipt of goods from suppliers.

Deputies have to ask hard questions about resources in relation to curriculum. For example:

- what evidence will the subject leader provide that a given sum will improve the performance of students?
- are there cheaper, but equally effective, ways of delivering this curriculum?
- would increased spending on low-cost support staff be more effective than provision of more time from high-cost teaching staff?
- are staff in the subject departments carrying out tasks that should be done by non-teachers?
- would IT provide a means for making a process such as recording less time consuming?

The deputy has another key role to play in curriculum development: the role of being the person who encourages staff members to articulate the theoretical underpinning of what they are intending to do. It is, unfortunately, all too common among teachers to underplay the role of 'theory' and de-value it. Indeed, this is one reason why the public and politicians find it so easy to be critical of what teachers do. Teachers need to develop a sound theoretical and research base for their work – about how to teach, and why they teach in particular ways, about what is included in the curriculum and what its value is, and so on. The job of the deputy is to ask the *why?* questions, and to demand answers that are increasingly reflective.

This last point leads neatly into the final section of this chapter, about the role of the deputy head as the leader of professional development activities within the school. This role is intimately connected to curriculum leadership, but is also wider in that it embraces the broader issues of pedagogical skills, and of professionalism generally.

——— Continuing professional development ———

The deputy head is often the person who is entrusted with the role of organising professional development within the school. Here we will look briefly at some key skills for doing this job effectively.

The starting point for professional development in a school has to be in establishing what is needed, and there are a number of ways in which this process can take place:

- through the appraisal system (this is dealt with in Chapter 11)
- through a trawl of staff opinion about needs
- through an analysis of the school's performance and areas of weakness
- through the head's and deputy's intentions for school development (for example, as set out in the School Development Plan)
- through Ofsted reports and findings.

An essential concept in providing continuing professional development is coherence. The use of the in-service budget must deliver those activities, for the whole staff or for individuals, that target areas ripe for improvement and further the school's overall effectiveness.

Continuing professional development is a topic vast enough for a book in its own right, and only the most basic guidance can be provided in a few pages. We have therefore chosen to try to achieve this through the use of tables and checklists that a busy deputy can use when trying to maintain quality professional development in the school.

TABLE 7.3 In-house professional development

In-house professional development might include any of the following:

- mentoring of inexperienced colleagues by more experienced
- role trading to enhance experience
- presentations by school staff on specific issues
- inter-school co-operation (role trading, sharing expertise)
- policy writing
- revising curriculum intentions and content
- exhibitions by commercial companies, demonstrations of new products.

TABLE 7.4 Setting up an input from a speaker

- brief the speaker fully about the school – its nature, staffing, location
- suggest that the speaker breaks up a long presentation with activities or a question time
- make proper arrangements – send a map, advise on a hotel if required, suggest how long local travel times will be, provide a parking space, and so on
- find out if the speaker will need materials reproduced in advance, what the equipment requirements are
- before the speaker arrives, lay out the furniture and set up any audiovisual equipment – make sure it is working!
- welcome the speaker on arrival, provide coffee, indicate the layout of the building
- give the speaker time to prepare for the input
- don't 'set the speaker up', e.g. bring the speaker into a controversial situation without warning
- at lunch or coffee breaks, make sure that the speaker is not abandoned and ignored
- allow an opportunity for follow-up at the end of the day.

TABLE 7.5 Using outside experts effectively

- choose the provider wisely
- know what you want from the provider and negotiate your programme
- facilitate their input – make sure they have what they need (*see* Table 7.4)
- prepare the staff – brief them, publish the intentions, give pre-reading etc.
- agree the learning outcomes for the day
- circulate a programme in advance
- keep to time!
- don't pack too much in – pace the event intelligently
- ambience is important – create the right mood
- venue can be important, though luxury is not
- make sure the headteacher is present all day
- leave some time for evaluation
- decide about any follow-up activities
- pay the bill promptly and say thank you to the visitor.

TABLE 7.6 Judging the effectiveness of professional development

The following criteria can be adapted and applied to a single event or over time to a professional development programme:

- are the intentions clear?
- is the event/programme relevant to needs?
- are the rationale and structure of the event/programme appropriate?
- are the learning methods appropriate to adults?
- does the event/programme improve school morale/culture?
- does it increase openness to ideas?
- has it met teachers' needs?
- are there opportunities for accreditation of the programme?
- is professional confidence increased?
- is school management improved?
- is the work of the participants recorded or logged – is there a record of professional development for individual staff?
- does student learning improve?

TABLE 7.7 Possible Ofsted criteria for judging a school's professional development

What might Ofsted inspectors look for in a professional development programme for a school?

- evidence that staff/school needs are trawled and then met
- evidence that the professional development is appropriate to the development of the school
- consistency between what the school identifies for development and the training it plans and uses to reach those goals
- evidence of effective co-ordination of the programme
- evidence of value in terms of learning gains for students
- evidence of overall 'value for money'
- evidence of the content and quality of the training programmes
- evidence that training days are used effectively
- evidence that 'eligible others' (e.g. governors, support staff) are included.

Summary

This chapter has dealt with matters that are at the very heart of the school and its effectiveness, and has emphasised the very real part that an effective deputy head can play in increasing that effectiveness. It is precisely because the role of the deputy head is so vital that it is worthy of a book of skills such as the present volume.

Our intention is that, at the end of this chapter, you will have:

- considered the relative roles and importance of teaching and learning
- looked carefully at why and how to monitor staff and observe teaching
- made yourself conversant with any deficiencies in your understanding of the whole school curriculum
- adopted sound strategies for ensuring high quality continuing professional development within your school.

Dealing with parents and governors

O ne omnipresent aspect of the deputy head's role is dealing with people. This chapter looks at two important groups of people with whom the deputy may be continually involved: parents and governors. The chapter begins with relations with parents.

——— Dealing with parents ———

The deputy's dealings with parents can take many forms:

- face to face
- in writing
- formal
- informal
- in relation to routine matters (e.g. providing advice or information)
- in relation to a crisis.

This chapter concentrates on the skills needed in face-to-face meetings. Written communications are dealt with in Chapter 13.

——— Face-to-face meetings ——— with parents

Meetings in relation to routine matters often cast the deputy in the role of the counsellor. Take the following possible scenario.

CASE STUDY

Jake's thing

Jake is a pleasant boy who has created no problems since he joined the school two years ago. His parents have always been supportive of the school without being greatly in evidence at school functions. Jake has an older brother and a younger sister. His school work has always been above average, but has never signalled that he is likely to be a high-flier. Suddenly he has become moody, depressed even. He has shown a couple of instances of resistance to instructions from teachers, and has been mildly aggressive to class-mates. His teacher has tried to speak informally to him about these changes, but she has met with silence from him or assurances that everything is 'OK'. Then you get a phone call from the parents requesting an interview.

This situation – a vague change of behaviour from conformist to mild deviance – is not unknown among young people, of course. You don't know what to expect from the parents: in making the appointment with the school administrator they did not indicate if they were coming to communicate information or to seek advice. You have to prepare your mind for the interview, and for your strategy at the initial stages. What would you do?

TASK 22

Interviewing parents: preparation

What would you do to prepare yourself for the interview with Jake's parents?

Make a list of the tasks you would need to undertake in order to be ready to meet them.

There is a cautionary tale (a true one) about such a meeting.

CASE STUDY

Finding the right word

The pupil in question was Michael, a bit of a live wire and sometimes disruptive. He was a primary pupil, and was required to communicate 'news' to the teacher as part of 'sharing time'. He did so, along with everyone else.

As luck would have it, Michael's mum wanted to take Michael out of school for a day to attend a very special family event. Rather than write a note, she arranged to see the deputy to explain the situation in person. When she arrived for the appointment, she was a little disconcerted to be given what appeared to her to be an unnecessarily solicitous welcome and to be shown to the head's private office.

The deputy arrived, rather flustered, and went nervously into a stream of conversation that went like this:

'I'm so glad you felt you were able to come and talk to us, Mrs Smith. We are all very sympathetic, and quite understand. Now, if there's anything we can do, don't hesitate to ask. We do keep a stock of spare clothes here, you know, if money gets tight. And of course we'll understand if Michael doesn't always make it punctually to school ...'

Mrs Smith mumbled something about having only come to ask about a wedding. The deputy stopped dead.

'What did you think I'd come about?' asked Mrs Smith.

'Oh,' said the deputy, 'We all assumed it was Michael's "news".'

'What precisely was this news?' asked a confused Mrs Smith.

'Well,' replied the deputy. 'His class teacher got them talking about their dads the other day, and he told us.'

'Told you?'

'Yes. You know ... That he's an alcoholic.'

Mr Smith was a wine buyer for a City company. But Michael hadn't quite mastered the vocabulary.

This case suggests that, in preparing for any parental interview, the first rule ought always to be:

Listen first; talk second.

For the pastoral or advisory interview, then, the guidelines in Table 8.1 might be helpful.

Problem solving with parents

Sometimes parents seek an interview because they are angry or frustrated about some aspect of school life. At other times the school must seek the interview to elicit parental support with a difficult student. These interviews contain actual or potential conflict and may call for serious negotiating skills.

TABLE 8.1	Guidelines for pastoral or advisory interviews with parents

- ensure that parents are welcomed when they arrive

- an offer of tea or coffee may help put them at ease

- seat them in a quiet waiting area where they will not be under scrutiny

- don't keep them waiting longer than necessary

- conduct your conversation in a private place

- begin by establishing what they have come about

- often, the real reason will not be the first declared reason, so use questions to probe under the surface of the situation

- once you are happy you have established the real issues, try to discover what they want to achieve through the meeting

- if possible, meet their aspirations

- if not, negotiate new ones

- in a long meeting, summarise progress from time to time

- at the end, rehearse agreements

- follow up meetings with a letter that records the outcomes

- where necessary, move to a further cycle of talking with the child, with the parents again, and with all of them together if necessary

- involve other professionals, with agreement, if appropriate.

Of course, your aim in such interviews must be to maintain the requirements of the school; but within those parameters you may wish to achieve a solution to the problem that is seen as acceptable to both parties. The guiding principles for such interviews might include:

- the need to try to defuse the conflict element in the encounter

- the need to persuade the parents that what you want to achieve is a solution, not a victory

- the need to convince the parents of the fact that both parties (they and the school) should be on the same side

- the need to demonstrate that, at the end, everyone has won.

CASE STUDY

Conflict zone

A senior student was taking a vocational course in the sixth form. She and the tutor did not have a good working relationship. The tutor told Elizabeth that her standards were not high enough and that she would not enter her for the assessment. She had to repeat the course. To complicate matters, Elizabeth's mother was qualified in the subject of the course, and had a genuine (if slightly dated) knowledge of the requirements. Elizabeth's parents were angered by the tutor's decision, and demanded to see the deputy head. When they arrived they were very angry and upset. The father threatened violence.

How would you deal with this?

TASK 23

Dealing with a difficult interview with parents

Study the case above.

What steps might you take to defuse this situation?

What line might you take to try to be fair to, and to satisfy, all parties: Elizabeth, the tutor and the parents?

How do you think you might feel in this situation?

Have you had to handle difficult situations like this already? What happened?

In the case reported above, the deputy acted as follows. (Since there are no right or wrong answers to handling problems of human relations, you might have handled it differently and still been successful.)

The deputy first had to deal with the threat of violence. He judged that it was intended, but not imminent. So he pointed out to the father that the school secretary was next door and that one tap of the intercom button would mean that the police would be involved. (Bluff: there was no intercom.) He suggested that they should try reason first since he, like Elizabeth's parents, was concerned first and foremost with the very best for Elizabeth as for all students, and that a good solution for her should be the priority.

This defused the situation enough for the deputy to go on and ask the parents to list all the issues as they saw them, while he wrote them down. He promised that, when this was completed, he would deal with each in turn, and that they could revisit them all for a fuller discussion.

The main issues whittled down to two concerns:

1 Whether Elizabeth's performance was really that bad.

2 Elizabeth's relationship with the course tutor.

The deputy established that Elizabeth was one of a small group of students who had under-performed. He explained that the course tutor had already informed the exam board of the candidates to be entered this year, so the situation was out of his hands in that sense. This angered the parents, and he had to act quickly to defuse the situation again. He suggested that Elizabeth, along with the other non-exam entrants, should repeat their year with the aim of gaining much higher pass marks than had seemed likely this year. This was a nuisance for them, but would be in their ultimate best interests. He suggested that, since there was no conflict between the 'repeat' students and other tutors, they should join the main body of the students for all sessions except those conducted by the course tutor. To cater for the needs of the 'repeats' like Elizabeth, he undertook to make alternative teaching arrangements for the section of the course normally delivered by the course tutor; but he insisted that he would meet this group and spell out to them that – as an older cohort – they had to take much more responsibility for their own learning. They would be treated like adults, but have to act like it. They would undertake some private study, but would have to give guarantees of commitment.

He gained the agreement of the parents to this, only then moving on to look at the problems with the course tutor herself. He trod a careful path to explain why the tutor's judgement may have been sound, but he undertook to monitor relations between the course tutor and all the students in the group to explore whether the parents' fears of bias were justified. (He actually believed from his previous knowledge of the situation that they were.) He also established that Elizabeth was not always tractable at home, and that the course tutor may have had genuine difficulties with her.

He offered to meet the parents at any time if they felt they had a problem, and asked them to contact him personally if there was any difficulty in the future. Meanwhile, he would speak to Elizabeth at regular intervals and check on her progress over the next year, but always within the context that much was now being expected of her.

The interview ended amicably, in contrast to the way in which it had begun.

Conclusion

The kind of outcome described in the factual scenario above makes the problem-solving approach look easy. It isn't. Theorists describe three possible outcomes to such interviews:

- win–win – in which both parties feel satisfied with the outcome of the meeting.

- win–lose – in which one party insists on their own way, and the other is defeated. This is, by definition, pretty undesirable, since if the school loses it opens the floodgates of conflict with other parents, and if the parents lose they are aggrieved and their youngsters will remain disaffected (or be withdrawn).

- lose–lose – in which both parties end up blocking a positive outcome (win–win) so that they do not lose face.

Further interesting analysis of negotiating skills can be found in Jane Hodgson's book *Thinking on Your Feet in Negotiations* (1996), though the material is taken from the world of business rather than education. The material in this chapter has not exhausted the ways in which parents and the deputy interact. Other sections of the book deal with public relations generally, and with home–school written communication.

———— The deputy and the governors ————

The relationship between the deputy and the governors is a difficult topic to deal with. The crux of the problem lies in the idiosyncrasies of how individual schools operate. Any of the following apply:

- the deputy may be a staff member of the governing body
- the deputy may not be a staff member of the governing body
- the deputy may attend the governing body as an observer
- the deputy may not be allowed to attend as an observer
- the deputy may or may not attend governors' committees such as Policy or Finance and General Purposes
- the deputy may advise governors' committees such as the Policy Committee
- in primary schools, parent governors may be seen daily at the school gate and may assist in classrooms
- in secondary schools neither of these will apply: the governors may be infrequent visitors to the school or always deal directly with the head.

Nevertheless, some basic suggestions can be made about how the deputy can relate to governors.

Organising visits to the school

The deputy, with the head's agreement, can be proactive in organising visits by governors to the school or in making special arrangements for them at regular events such as parents' evening or school performances. It is also important that the deputy considers the public relations aspects of the role in relation to governors: knowing their names, welcoming them when they come on site, facilitating their needs when they want to see aspects of the school in action, and so on. The deputy will also need to be tactful in some situations, perhaps to steer individual governors away from usurping the roles of inspectors. It may be possible to encourage governors from the local business community to give tangible support to school projects. A deputy might well be involved in all these tasks.

Deputising for the head

One difficult role is to deputise for the head at governors' meetings should the head be absent. This is more difficult in situations where the deputy is not normally a member or observer at governors' meetings, since there will be some unfamiliarity with procedure. In some schools the head is a frequent absentee, through sickness or through demand by outside agencies for his/her particular skills on a consultancy basis.

Piggy in the middle

Many of the deputies who contributed ideas to this book characterised their role *vis-à-vis* governors as 'piggy in the middle' (just as it is for many in relation to the head), i.e. they have to represent the views of the staff to the governors, and the views of the governors to the staff. This 'Janus' role of looking both ways at once is one that many deputies find hard or even stressful.

Reporting to governors

The other major role that our deputies had in relation to governors was in presenting reports (oral or written) to them. The skills of oral and written reporting are dealt with in Chapter 13.

Conclusion

In conversations with deputies about governors some words – such as 'ambiguity', 'undefined' – kept cropping up. Deputies may find that they are not party to governing body meetings while some relatively junior staff are members of the governing body. Some governing bodies brief all the staff about the outcomes of their meetings, others do not, so a deputy may be quite ignorant of the governance of the school.

In short, this is a tricky area, and the best advice has to be: if possible, become involved in the governing body and its work, and stay within the limits of your knowledge.

—————— Summary ——————

Our intention is that, at the end of this chapter, you will have:

- become aware of some pitfalls in dealing with parents
- adopted good procedures for face-to-face contact with parents
- begun to consider your role in relation to school governors
- thought through some ways to relate to school governors effectively.

Standards and quality

It has been implied already that much of this book is in fact about quality and improving quality in the broadest sense. In this chapter we intend to discuss an approach to quality based on the theoretical model of total quality management (TQM), and to apply this model to assessing school standards based on TQM principles.

Total quality management

TQM is based on principles that were generated in a business environment. Simply put, TQM looks at an organisation from the point of view of its customers and clients. The customers and clients of the school can be held to include:

- the students
- the teachers
- parents and prospective parents
- past parents and students
- governors
- the local community members
- the LEA
- the DfEE.

Each of these client groups has a legitimate set of expectations that they might reasonably expect to be fulfilled, as set out in Table 9.1.

Thus TQM puts customers or clients at the heart of its process and allows them to define what quality is. In this way, quality becomes meeting the needs, requirements and standards that the client defines as necessary. TQM emphasises a process of continuous improvement in which those responsible for delivering quality are proactive rather than reactive.

But this responsibility is not confined to senior managers, even though they may oversee the process. Everyone, without exception – which in a school means teachers, students, non-teaching support staff, dinner supervisors, cooks and caretakers – has an equal responsibility for delivering quality in those aspects of the school's functioning in which they are involved. The quality delivered is measured: both statistical and non-statistical methods may be used.

TABLE 9.1 Clients and their expectations

Client group	Some expectations
The students	Interesting lessons, a safe and conducive learning ethos, and the chance to gain good grades
The teachers	Reasonable working conditions and consultation on appropriate issues
Parents and prospective parents	Good information about the school and high standards of performance and behaviour
Past parents and students	Knowledge that the school values their opinions about their/children's experiences
Governors	Integration into the life of the school; sound data on which to base their discussions
The local community members	Sound behaviour from the students outside school
The LEA	Return of school-based data and other forms of communication
The DfEE	Efforts to improve students' performance to meet national norms

One significant aspect of this 'total quality' is in terms of the human relations that operate within the school, and work is often seen as collaborative and team oriented. It goes without saying that such quality depends on the value placed on every participant and on the training given to them to help them maintain quality. Every aspect and decision relating to the life of the organisation is measured against the quality criteria.

Defining the mission and intentions of the school

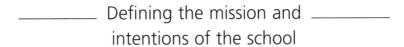

One place at which to begin this process is to define the mission of the school. Most schools now have a 'mission statement' or something akin to it. For example, here are two we discovered in our research for this book:

> *At Franklin School our aim is to provide the best for our students and to seek to draw out their best in work and respect for others.*
>
> *Our mission is summed up thus: Act enterprisingly, work in partnership, achieve excellence.*

Even existing statements need periodic review to see whether they are working and whether they are still relevant. The key to defining and then sustaining the mission of an institution is to involve all the stakeholders in the process.

Having a clear mission or a vision of where the school is going is an important factor in quality; but ensuring that the vision is shared is vital. Quality is one of the things that 'sells' a school. But the school has not only to be marketed to the external clientele: the prospective parents and students, members of the local community. The school must equally be 'sold' to the 'internal market', i.e. to its current students, teaching and non-teaching staff, and existing parents. These internal clients of the school have to develop a pride of ownership. The founder of TQM, A.V. Feigenbaum, summed it up in statements like:

> *Quality requires continuous improvement*
>
> *Quality is a way of managing*
>
> *Quality is an ethic*
>
> *Quality requires both individual and team zealotry*
>
> (n.d. *The Quality Gurus*, London: Department of Trade & Industry)

As a deputy you will have a role in sustaining the quality of the school and its operations and, while it may well not be your responsibility to oversee the total production of the school's mission statement or vision for the future, you will have a hand in the process of sustaining the school's intentions and keeping up staff morale. So it might be worthwhile to review your mission statement for your own purposes from time to time.

These are some characteristics of effective mission statements:

- they relate the school to its context
- they put clients at the centre
- they are brief and businesslike
- they are expressed in clear language
- they are negotiated with, and owned by, all staff and other relevant parties

- they identify clear targets
- they provide intermediate steps on the road to success
- they are achievable.

TASK 24

Reviewing your mission statement

Take a long, dispassionate look at the intentions of your school as they are summarised in your mission statement.

Ask yourself some key questions:

- does this statement reflect accurately the current intentions of the school?
- is the school achieving these intentions?
- if not, why not?
- has the school reached the targets set in the mission – is it time to move on?
- does the statement enshrine the principles of quality discussed earlier in the chapter?
- if not, where does it fall short and what needs to be done about it?
- what is the next priority and how can it be achieved?

From principle to policy

Once the overall intentions and vision of the school are defined, the perspective has to shift to the delivery of those intentions. The starting point for this process is in formulating policy about individual areas of school life.

Some policies are statutorily required: for example, those for special educational needs. Others are optional, but are nevertheless subject to quite close scrutiny by outside agencies such as Ofsted. A school might reasonably be expected to have policies about the following issues.

Generic matters

- attendance and absence
- behaviour
- bullying

- sex education
- dealing with queries from parents
- school uniform and equipment
- out-of-school visits, activities
- supervision of students outside the classroom (e.g. in the playground)
- provision for students/parents from ethnic minority cultures.

Curriculum matters

- teaching and learning
- the whole curriculum
- the parts of curriculum not covered by the National Curriculum
- each National Curriculum area
- assessment, recording and reporting
- special educational needs
- teaching the most able
- homework.

Financial matters

- guidance to budget holders
- ordering systems
- stocktaking and audit.

These are just some of the areas on which there may be policies. Sometimes such policies are long and rather convoluted. So what constitutes a good policy? There are some basic requirements that every policy needs, and these are shown as Table 9.2.

TABLE 9.2 Elements in a good policy

1 Rationale: The policy needs to set out the background to the issue, to set the scene and spell out the underlying philosophy. It should do this in an uncomplicated way and quite briefly.

2 Intentions: The policy should then set out the school's intentions to deal with the issue concerned. It will set out what the school would expect to happen as a model of good practice.

3 Relation of the policy to other policies: Policies across the school should achieve internal coherence, in other words they should all be directed to the overall mission and ethos of the school. The relationship of any one policy to other relevant policies, and to these overall intentions, should be identified. For example, in a policy on bullying it might be appropriate to refer to the mission of the school as a place of physical and psychological security, and also to the behaviour policy in relation to the general standards expected of students.

4 Strategies for overseeing the policy: This section deals with how the policy will be monitored and who will do the monitoring.

5 Issues regarding implementation: Here the policy is concerned with who will implement the policy and how it will be put into practice. For example, in a policy on a National Curriculum subject area, the document may lay down the roles and responsibilities for the Head of Geography/the Geography co-ordinator, and for all those who teach the subject.

6 The resource base: This section examines the human and material needs in order to implement the policy effectively.

7 Monitoring progress: A policy document should contain targets against timescales so that progress towards success can be assessed.

8 Evaluation of policy intentions: As well as looking at whether those charged with implementing policy are succeeding, there should be an opportunity, planned for and built into the policy itself, for stocktaking on whether the policy intentions themselves are up to date and effective. This may imply a school-wide stage.

9 A cycle of review.

Governors and quality

Good policies do not, of themselves, ensure quality – though they are a step along the road. This chapter has stressed that, in ensuring quality, the clients should be at the centre of the process and that everyone involved in the school has a role to play, but there is one group to whom the law gives special responsibilities in overseeing quality: the governors of the school. It is worth pausing, therefore, to remind ourselves of precisely how the Government sees the role of the governing body.

In a publication called *Governing Bodies and Effective Schools* (DFE, 1995, p. 2), the three key roles were set out as follows:

■ to provide a strategic review

- to act as a critical friend
- to ensure accountability.

In looking at the school's mission or intentions, and in examining the process of drawing up policy, we have looked at the first of these issues – strategic review – from the school's perspective. From a governor's perspective, the process is encapsulated in seven questions that together sum up the role of critical friend (based on DFE (1995), p. 4):

- where are we trying to get to?
- where are we now?
- how can we get from where we are to where we want to be?
- what are the priorities in this process?
- what resources have we got?
- who is responsible for doing what, by when?
- how will we know/be able to judge whether the goals have been achieved?

The third governor role is that of ensuring accountability from the school, an issue dealt with later in this chapter.

Planning for quality: the School Development Plan

In this section we turn our intention away from the governors as critical friends and external monitors of quality and back to the heart of the school. The intentions of the school are operationalised by its employees through the School Development Plan (SDP). Tables 9.3 and 9.4 show extracts (only) from a primary and a secondary SDP. These are meant to be typical rather than exemplary.

Note that in these plans the deputy plays a number of important roles:

- as planning officer, drawing up sections of the plan
- as co-ordinator, making sure that some aspects of the plan are achieved
- as budget holder, responsible for resourcing parts of the plan
- as executive, carrying through some of the plan's intentions and reporting on them.

The deputy probably plays a wider range of roles in relation to school development planning than does any other member of staff. While the school policies set out the mission of the school and are the public face of the school's intentions, the SDP is the means by which members of the school staff are mobilised into achieving those intentions.

TABLE 9.3 Extract from a primary school development plan

Task	Timescale	What to do	By whom?	Cost
Overhaul English policy	end of term 2	1. Discuss with English staff	Deputy	zero
	end of term 3	2. Present policy to governors for approval	Head	zero
Organise school field trip	end of term 1	Contact outward bound centre and make booking	Deputy	zero
	On booking	Raise and pay invoice	Secretary	est. £550
	1st March	Letter to parents	Deputy	postage
	end of term 2	Prepare worksheets	Subject staff	repro cost

TABLE 9.4 Extract from secondary school development plan

4.9 Experimental approaches to teaching and learning

During the current academic year it is the intention of the school to explore the possibilities of teaching some of its GCE A level courses using distance learning materials developed in the school. These materials will be computer-based, and will be available through the school's Intranet. The deputy head, Dr Spock, will be responsible for the overall direction of the scheme, which will operate as follows:

■ the intention of the scheme is to make savings of 40% in the cost of delivering A level courses, initially in Geography, History and English. It is important to ensure that quality of teaching and of student results do not suffer and may even be improved;

- Dr Spock will form a planning team of key personnel from each of the named departments, augmented with ICT staff;

- Dr Spock will facilitate staff release, using the cover budget, to enable suitable materials to be prepared (by 1st March). Named personnel from each department will be responsible for co-ordinating departmental resource production;

- ICT staff, under the leadership of the Chief Technical Officer, will operationalize the materials and see that systems are up and running for trial by 1st June. The Bursar will provide a budget of £5,000 to finance the experimental stages of the programme;

- Dr Spock will arrange for the programme to be monitored by a member of Startreck University so that the scheme can be effectively evaluated;

- a report to the governors will be drawn up by Dr Spock and presented by the Head Teacher in July. Subject to the success of the scheme and the approval of governors the scheme will be brought on stream from September next.

In later chapters we deal with the deputy as a budget officer and with the skill of reporting, e.g. to a governing body. Here the concentration is on the planning process to ensure that the plan itself reflects the 'total quality' aspirations set out in this chapter.

In compiling an SDP, one important factor is the extent to which its content and intentions are taken on board by the school staff – teachers and paraprofessionals. As someone involved in the compilation of the plan, the deputy often assumes this consultation role or participates in the consultation process. TQM demands that all relevant parties are fully involved in the initial consultation and are then fully committed to the outcome.

With this in mind, you might consider how you would deal with the situation in Task 25.

TASK 25

Quality in delivering a National Curriculum subject

History is currently in a difficult position in the school because there is a staff vacancy for the subject co-ordinator/head of department role. You are asked to lead its development for six months, though you are not an historian. Three staff teach history. There is a policy, but you suspect it may be out of tune with the National Curriculum requirements. Teaching methods are an unknown quantity.

Work in students' notebooks relies on textbook sources only. One member of staff is known to be 'difficult'.

- what would you need to find out?
- how would you find these things out?
- who would you need to consult? About what?
- what would you need to do?
- how would you set about doing these things?
- what kind of a timed/sequenced plan would you put in place for the next six months?
- how would you use your knowledge in helping to appoint a new subject leader for history?

Monitoring and evaluating quality

So far in this chapter the emphasis has been on building quality into what happens in the school. Here the scene changes to trying to discover whether quality has been achieved. We are moving into the realm of controversy, of course, because different groups will have different ideas about what constitute appropriate ways to monitor and evaluate. Some will demand definitions of the elusive goal: quality. Others will introduce the concept of 'value added'. We need to begin by clarifying some of these issues.

Quality: a definition

The good news is that there is less of a problem with defining quality than one might imagine. In fact, we have already defined it. First, we have said that quality is what the clients define it as – and we took their views into account in compiling the overall intentions and mission for the school. Second, in breaking down the overall intentions of the school into component parts – policies – we have again defined the quality we want to achieve within each of those parts through the rationale and intentions of the individual policies and through the school's development planning. Thus the definitions of quality are already embedded in what we have stated as our intentions at each stage of the strategic planning process.

Value added

The concept of value added is equally easily defined (if not measured). It is the assessment of how much of the journey from 'where we are now' to 'where we want to be' has been completed. So when compiling the mission statement or formulating the policy, we took stock of the present as it then was. When we then review those items at a later date, the 'value added' is the journey from that baseline to the moment of review.

 Consider these examples:

- a student is baseline tested on entry to school and then tested again at Key Stage 1. The difference in performance is the value added in learning achievement for that student;

- a school has six exclusions for bullying in a year as a result of 21 incidents of bullying. Worried by this, the staff and governors develop a new bullying policy and implement it in the school. In the following year incidents of bullying have dropped by 67 per cent and there have been only two cases serious enough to warrant exclusion. The value added can be easily assessed;

- the parents of a student with a mobility problem approach the school for a place. The school has no suitable access routes for a wheelchair. However, the governors decide to spend some capitation on ramps and a stair lift. As a result, this student and two other local youngsters can now use the school rather than travel long distances to another school by taxi. Value has been added for the affected students, for their parents and to the school plant.

The monitoring and evaluation process: being accountable

A leading role in the monitoring and evaluation process may be assumed by the governors of the school. (Some governing bodies are not strong on fulfilling this aspect of their role, but they are now decreasing in proportion to the total number of governing bodies. Where the governors do not do this it must, nevertheless, be done in house by the head, deputy and staff, and governors should be encouraged to take part and learn from the experience.) If the governors do take the lead, then they should be asking the following key questions (DFE, 1995, p. 3):

- how is our school currently performing?
- are some parts of the school more effective than others? If so, why?
- are some groups of students doing better than others? If so, why?

- how does the school's achievement now compare with past achievement?

- how does the school's performance compare with that of other schools?

_____ Accountable for what? _____
What to monitor and evaluate

The really important question is: what kinds of things should be subject to the kind of 'quality audit' that we have been describing in this chapter? The answer can be surprisingly detailed, but some of the factors you might like to include are listed in Table 9.5.

TABLE 9.5 Some factors that may be included in a quality audit

- test results: National Curriculum tests and external examination results

- assessment procedures

- methods of recording and reporting

- attendance rates

- exclusions

- level of demand for admission to the school

- levels and range of extra-curricular provision and participation

- student behaviour and attitudes

- gender issues and equal opportunities

- provision for students from different ethnic backgrounds

- ways in which the school meets special educational needs at all levels

- provision for the more able – helping all students to reach their full potential

- relative success of individual subject areas

- behaviour around the school

- level of satisfaction with the school by parents

- staff morale and commitment

- professionalism and professional behaviour of teachers and support staff (paraprofessionals) across the school

- quality of teaching

- variety of teaching and learning styles

- appropriateness of staffing to the school's policies and intentions

- data systems and their use to bring about improvements in the school

- communication structures within the school

- use of information and communications technology

- value for money in using the school's budget

- the facilities provided by the school plant – for learning and relaxation

- issues of value added

- community views of the school

- customer satisfaction

- extent to which school targets in SDP and policies are being met.

_____ Statistical monitoring _____

Most people would probably see statistical monitoring as relating only to keeping track of students' progress in examinations or tests. This is a worthwhile process, because it does measure what learning is taking place. Such measures are often regarded as crude, but used in conjunction with other statistical and non-statistical data they can be informative and may point up trends in the school.

Task 26 asks you to draw up a pro forma on which you might collect statistical data about the performance of students in your school.

TASK 26 _____

Drawing up a pro forma to collect statistical data

You wish to monitor the progress of students through your school in terms of their measured learning gains and achievements, and to draw some 'value added' conclusions.

Compile a pro forma that will contain:

1 Baseline assessment data for each student on entry to the school.

2 Performance data for each student at each stage of formal assessment (Key Stages 1 and 2 for the primary sector; Key Stages 3 and 4 for the secondary sector).

Now go on to interrogate the data you have collected:

- what does it tell you about the general level of progress across the school – the value added?

- are there areas of unusually good or unsatisfactory progress?

- what are these?

- how can you establish the causes of these?

- what conclusions can you draw from the data about management decisions that need to be taken in order to improve the school's overall quality of performance?

Using statistical data to monitor learning gains through examination results is relatively easy to do, but schools are about more than examination results. However, other quality indicators can also be collected using statistical means. In one school we visited, for example, there is a monthly 'management information pack' produced by the senior managers for all staff. This contains entries such as those in Table 9.6.

TABLE 9.6 Management information data, June 1999

Attendance:

Year	Roll	Attendance rate
7	250	94%
8	207	96%
9	231	94%
10	205	92%
11	221	91%
12	131	97%
13	95	97%

Other kinds of data about the school that might be collected by statistical means, and thus monitored for trends, would include teaching staff and support staff absence, the amount of time spent on professional development activities by these groups, information about special needs (such as statementing), health and safety incidents, extra-curricular activities, school team results, and so on.

Statistical analysis is a particular skill that will aid a deputy in monitoring progress and quality in the school, when applied to appropriate activities.

The role of the deputy in monitoring and evaluating

The deputy is an important figure in maintaining the quality of what happens in school. In touch with the head and the staff, still with some teaching responsibilities and with a brief for many aspects of administration and organisation, the deputy provides a comprehensive and unique view of the school. But it behoves the deputy to remember an important insight into the business of maintaining quality in the school:

> *Quality improvement is a never-ending journey.*
>
> (Tom Peters)

James Champy, a world expert in a management approach called reengineering, makes this statement:

> *We have to abandon the management credo 'Get it right, then keep it going' and embrace the credo 'Get it right, and make it better, and better, and better' or even 'Make it something else'. We must give up the comforting illusion that there is one conclusive solution to any business (or human) problem, and live with the fact that each problem changes virtually overnight, and no two problems are exactly the same, that many problems can only be coped with.*
>
> (Champy, 1995, p. 27)

Therefore, the deputy must learn a range of skills to enable the role of quality controller to be played well amidst this insecurity. Among these skills might be:

- observational skills: the ability to observe, formally, the quality of learning and teaching across the school;
- people skills: to get staff, students and others to work together and in teams and to support them in their work;
- communication skills: in helping to convey the vision for the school;
- analytical skills: to absorb, sift, interpret and refine information;
- statistical skills: to manipulate and interpret school-related data;
- financial skills: to budget and stay within budget.

These skills are, or have been, dealt with in this book, while the next skills to be discussed – in Chapter 10 – are in addition to these: the skills of the public relations and marketing officer.

———— Summary ————

Our intention is that, at the end of this chapter, you will have:

■ considered the value of approaches such as Total Quality Management

■ begun to define quality in relation specifically to your school

■ looked at the role of governors in quality assurance

■ thought through the key issues in school development planning

■ looked at a range of methods for monitoring and evaluating quality in schools.

External relations

In this chapter we shall look at two roles commonly played by deputy heads: the marketing officer and the public relations officer. We begin with a discussion about what marketing means when applied to schools.

——— Marketing the school ———

In the previous chapter we suggested that there are two markets. The external market consists of potential students and their parents, members of the local community, and those who have a professional role in relation to the school such as LEA officers and Ofsted inspectors. The internal market includes the school's current students, teaching and non-teaching staff, governors and current parents.

Marketing consists of managing the exchange between the school and its clients inside and outside the institution. It is a two-way process concerned with managing relationships through effective communication. Marketing is:

> *The means by which the school actively communicates and promotes its purpose, values and products to the pupils, parents, staff and wider community.*
>
> (Davies and Ellison, 1997, p. 204)

There tends to be cynicism among some teachers about language and activities that mirror a commercial environment too closely. Up to a point this is fair; we shall discuss why in a moment. But for now, let us pursue the metaphor.

Why should schools bother to market themselves? The answers are both idealistic and pragmatic:

- so that those with an interest can assess and appreciate the quality of the education offered by the school

- to attract and retain students, thereby benefiting from the revenue from formula funding

- to enhance the reputation of the school in the local community

- to maintain and increase market share of potential students.

Above all, the 'What?' questions about marketing the school must consist of conveying to a relevant audience messages about the quality of the institution. These include the successful learning that happens in the school, the calibre of the teaching, the effectiveness of the pastoral care for students, the range of and achievements in extra-curricular activities, and the desirability of the school culture and ethos.

Some teachers treat this approach with suspicion. They point to the 'sordid commercialism' of much of everyday life, and want to distance schools from it. They are afraid that they will simply follow the example of high-street traders, packaging ordinary goods in attractive wrapping, and thereby losing trust. They sneer at the 'have a nice day' mentality of some commercial outlets, and feel that the concept of the market is out of place in public service. These are understandable reactions. But the reality is that the trend in modern society is towards greater accountability, which in turn means that our 'services' have to be explained and justified in the public arena. This is wholly laudable, and to use some of the techniques of the marketplace to further that end is almost inevitable. The 1988 Education Act effectively made parents and students 'consumers', with powers of choice hitherto almost unprecedented, and thereby left schools without realistic options. So schools have to engage in marketing (communicating the benefits of the organisation) in order to have a share of the market (the means by which resources are allocated). That in turn makes teachers into marketing managers, and the deputy head often has to lead the marketing team.

The process of marketing requires that schools investigate their market (that is, undertake market research). This will assist them in developing a market strategy, which will itself be part of a wider strategic intent for the school. Strategic intent is the broad vision of where the school should be heading in the future. A school will succeed in achieving its strategic intentions, however, only to the extent that everyone in the internal market shares that vision and tries to implement it. The vision will be customer led, as we saw in the previous chapter, and will depend on everyone striving for – and marketing – the quality that the vision encompasses.

All of this is interesting theory, but how does this kind of marketing work in practice?

Marketing a school to increase the intake of bilingual students

A deputy with responsibility for marketing the school becomes aware that the school is increasingly being approached by parents of students whose first language is not English: bilingual students. Some of these students are reasonably fluent in the second language, others less so; likewise their parents. The increase results from demographic trends in the local area.

The deputy recognises a market niche that can be used to the advantage of the school. She undertakes some preliminary investigation and discovers that five such families are now moving into the immediate area of the school. Her reading about bilingual students suggests that the National Curriculum is failing to meet the needs of bilingual students, and that many schools, by ignoring the students' language repertoire, are acting as if their lives and identities were of little value.

The deputy sets out to establish the marketing principles of a school that would be seen to be attractive to bilingual students and their parents. She calls together some interested teachers within the school, and some outside experts from the LEA's support team. This small working group develops a list of marketing principles for such a school, which are expressed in a series of statements for the school brochure:

- this school believes actively in equal opportunities
- this school aims to develop all students fully
- this school responds positively to existing in a multicultural society
- this school looks to strengthen its community links
- this school has a positive view of every student's family and background
- the staff of this school have an awareness of, and value, cultural diversity
- this school values every student in their uniqueness.

The statements are discussed at a staff meeting and endorsed by the staff. The working group is invited to continue its work by setting out some principles that can be incorporated into a policy for bilingual students in the school. This they do, and these are the principles they generate:

FOR ALL STUDENTS:

- *this school values and develops every student's language repertoire*
- *this school increases language awareness across the whole curriculum*
- *this school accepts cultural diversity as a strength*
- *this school promotes communication across cultures*
- *this school combats racism and associated problems.*

FOR BILINGUAL STUDENTS:

- *this school supports the learning of bilingual students*
- *this school values the ethnicity of its bilingual students*
- *this school enters into partnership with the families and communities of its bilingual students*
- *this school promotes the intellectual development of its bilingual students*
- *this school is actively concerned for the welfare of its bilingual students.*

The principles articulated here are turned into policy and approved by the school's governors. The deputy arranges a professional development day to work over the implications of the new policy for the ways in which departments handle their work. Some resource implications emerge, and a sum is allocated from the budget to provide ancillary support for the youngsters who are now in the school. The LEA team provides some additional advice, help and translation facilities (so that the school can communicate with parents whose English is limited). These bilingual youngsters progress well.

One of the school governors takes a particular responsibility for liaison with the families of the bilingual students. Informal networks of communications also develop. The school builds trust with the parents and their communities, and they in turn contribute to the life of the school by helping the school to explain their culture and festivals. Soon the school discovers that bilingual students from beyond the immediate locality are attempting to gain entry to the school because of its reputation for concern.

Conveying messages: the school brochure

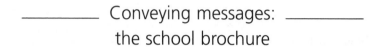

One of the jobs that the deputy head may well be asked to undertake is communication of messages about the school to the community through the production of the school brochure. This is an interesting task, but may well be a daunting one if such an undertaking is a new experience. As preparation, you might like to try Task 27.

TASK 27

Scrutinising school brochures

Collect together as many brochures from other schools as you can. You may obtain these, for example, from your own children's schools, from teaching colleagues in other schools, or by sending for them – even from other areas of the country. Try to collect at least a dozen so that you have a range of styles and types.

Work over each brochure, and try to decide on their strengths and weaknesses:

- what key messages do they convey?
- how well do they 'handle'?
- what formats work best?
- do pictures enhance the production? If so, what kind?
- which page layouts are most readable?
- what about type size/style?
- what is distinctive about each one? (And so on …).

Now look at your school's existing brochure. How does it compare/contrast?

What would need to be changed for it to be more effective?

Finally, seek out guidance about the things that are required by law to be included in the school brochure. Make sure you have all this basic data to hand before you start to compile anything (see Table 10.1).

Now that you have some idea about your own school brochure, and others, you can work through more systematically what you need to do to get your revised brochure off the ground.

In Chapter 13 we consider a different, team-based planning approach to the problem of revising the school brochure. Between these two chapters, you should have acquired all the tools you need to make an excellent job of this project.

TABLE 10.1 Legal requirements relating to school brochures

These are correct at the time of writing, but you should check the latest legislation, which will usually appear in governors' handbooks and is published by the DfEE.

- school name, address, telephone number. (You may want to add things like fax number, e-mail, maps.)
- name of the head teacher and the chair of governors
- the ethos and values of the school
- admissions information. School dates and hours for current year
- National Curriculum assessment results
- rates of authorised and unauthorised absence
- charging and remissions policy
- sex education policy. Religious education policy and arrangements, e.g. for special religious needs
- policy for dealing with complaints
- information about the curriculum and about special educational needs provision
- provision for sport

And in secondary schools:

- levels of applications to the school in previous years
- public examination results
- destinations of school leavers
- information about careers education and work experience facilities.

Here are some steps you can take to help you think the issues through:

- find the unique factors about your school that will make it attractive to potential consumers. This stage may have to be prefaced by some form of market research, however informal: you could ask students or members of the PTA, for example. Think about the educational aims of the school, any unique facilities, the successes of the school to date, the range of extra-curricular activities available, and any good publicity the school has received locally;

- the brochure will need to include the school's results in public tests and examinations, since this is obligatory. But you should think about what else makes the school successful: excellent drama or public performances, teachers who have outstanding skills, charity work, appearances on local or national radio and TV;

- decide on the overall style you are going to adopt for the brochure. A glance at a range of newspapers and magazines will indicate something of the variety of ways in which similar information can be presented. How will you package yours? Above all, remember what to avoid: over-intellectualism, obscure jargon or technical language, acronyms, in-jokes – in short, all the things that *exclude* people rather than include them;

- stress improvements made and plans for further improvements. Potential clients want to belong to a developing school, not one that rests merely on a glorious past. If the past was not glorious, how is it getting better?;

- review all the facilities of the school: are there any that are specially interesting or innovative? What would you be proud to show people? What image of the learning that takes place will be persuasive?;

- care for students is an important issue, too. Parents want to know, above all, that their children are being well looked after. Think about medical and counselling facilities, pastoral care organisation in the school, codes of behaviour, transport to school, canteen facilities, cloakrooms;

- now that the messages are beginning to take shape, you can go on to think about the production and design issues.

The quantity of text you use, and whether you want illustrations and photographs, in colour or black and white, will all affect the cost of the brochure. You may reject many of the options and produce something in-house, but attention to detail is still important. An in-house production may still use pictures scanned in to the computer, and you need to think about whether these should have borders and what kind. Small touches make a big difference.

Unless you have a good knowledge of this kind of activity, make an early visit to a local printer and get some quotes and examples of work. But always shop around with your final draft to get the best value. If you do use photographs, be very wary of utilising uncle Fred's instant (or even digital) camera and doing the job yourself. Professional photographers know how to create the messages you want. Most people are very uncritical in editing pictures, and the impact a good photographer can make is subliminal. One really outstanding image is better than a hundred average ones. The use of a school badge or logo is still a good thing: professional image makers would almost always advise against 'going modern' and doing away with it.

To summarise, the fundamental issues to come to grips with in production are:

1 What impact (through images) does your proposed brochure make?

2 Is the page layout easy to read?

3 Does the text convey the right messages?

4 Is the final format 'handle-able'?

5 Does the finished product have internal consistency and coherence of message?

Before leaving this topic, it might be worth drawing your attention to the fact that the school brochure is not the only means by which messages about the school may be conveyed. You may wish to consider how you could use:

- people (governors, PTA etc.) as conveyors of messages

- high-profile visitors

- other written material (letterheads, information sheets)

- in-house newsletters

- the media: newspapers, magazines, radio, TV

- advertising

- open evenings and other public events

- promotional video

- shop window displays (e.g. in the local estate agents).

The image of the school is conveyed in many different ways. Someone (and it may well be the deputy head) should have oversight of this process. There is plenty of scope for damage through sloppiness in this area, and the following are just some examples we have come across:

- letters to parents with incorrect grammar

- a spelling competition for which the information contained spelling errors

- open invitations to a carol concert that proved to be dramatically over-subscribed, leaving parents standing in corridors unable to see

- open evenings that were poorly organised so that parents queued several times for half an hour a time to see a staff member

- parents arriving for a school concert or event to find the location not signposted.

In this section we have assumed that the deputy is acting alone on this task. By contrast, in Chapter 13 a similar theme is tackled from a team perspective.

_____ Widening external relations: _____ the welcoming school

So far in this chapter we have considered the role of the deputy head in involving the internal market in embracing the vision for the school, in spelling out that vision, for example in attracting bilingual students into the school, and in providing public information in the form of the school brochure and by other means. The other area of responsibility that impinges on the external market and that may fall to the deputy to control is the way that staff within the school deal with people from outside the institution.

The telephone

The most obvious example of external relations is the telephone. It is often instructive to ring your own institution and assess how effectively your enquiry is dealt with and what ethos is conveyed. While we often parody the 'hotel chain' mentality of telephone answering (Good morning, this is Clinton's Hotel, my name is Monica, how can I help you?), the fact remains that such a response is at least basically polite and potentially helpful. The operative whose voice conveys boredom, and who simply obstructs any attempt to reach an answer to the enquirer's problems, is a menace. More clients are turned away by this than one is ever likely to discover.

So, _do_ have a strategy for answering the phone: agree with the secretarial staff and others what manner of greeting your school will offer. Here is some other helpful advice. The operative should:

- answer quickly (within, say, five rings)

- answer pleasantly

- have pen and paper ready

- use clear language, not jargon or 'put-offs'

- give undivided attention to the caller

- if transferring a call, make sure the caller does not have to repeat name, problem etc

- sound calm

- ask questions to prompt the caller if necessary

- if the call is a complaint, follow an agreed procedure (*see* below).

Complaints

Inevitably, the school will receive complaints. It is important to have a clear strategy for dealing with them. One business acquaintance of ours makes the following points about complaints:

- only 15 per cent of people with a problem complain

- more than 25 per cent of complainants have their problems resolved

- about 50 per cent of complainants will go elsewhere next time

- dissatisfied customers tell their friends, who tell their friends ...

- 95 per cent of those whose complaints are dealt with effectively will remain loyal

- satisfied former complainants are more loyal than those with no problems

- service is what makes the difference.

TASK 28

Deducing the messages about complaints for school procedures

Given the bullet points about complainants listed above, what are the messages that can be drawn by schools for handling complaints that may come from parents and others?

Write a brief (one side of A4) strategy paper about how the school should deal with complaints, and who should do what to resolve them.

In dealing with complaints there are some golden rules. It is important to listen and not to be defensive (the clients might be right!). Understand the client's viewpoint. Don't be afraid to admit error and apologise. Don't argue or pass the buck. Be helpful: find a positive outcome. Thank the client for raising the issue. Follow up the complaint some time later to make sure the client is still happy with the solution.

External relations are about professionalism, and it is useful to remember that some quite simple ploys will give confidence to clients. For example, always dress appropriately and encourage staff to do so. Schools are workshops in one sense, but scruffiness is no answer. Show pride in your job and a job well done. Be supportive of your colleagues and show respect for the clients. Give them the care and attention they deserve and encourage others to do the same. Use their names and make eye contact. Smile! Encourage others to make these approaches part of the school culture.

On the wall in our office we have the legend: 'Students do not interrupt our work, they are our work'. Similarly, every school should have as its watchword:

> *Clients (students, parents, governors, the community) are our work, they do not interrupt it.*

Summary

Our intention is that, at the end of this chapter, you will have:

- examined market philosophy as it relates to schools
- analysed the public face of your school, e.g. as it appears in the school brochure
- considered ways of improving this public face
- developed a system for handling complaints.

Mentoring, appraising and interviewing

The three topics that make up this chapter share some common characteristics. These will emerge as the chapter proceeds, but can be summarised by saying that they all depend on interpersonal skills.

___ Mentoring: wise counsellor or ___ the blind leading the blind?

Mentoring has become an accepted part of professional life in the twenty-first century. The chances are that, as a deputy head, you will have a mentor. You may even be asked to select this person yourself. Here we argue that for a mentor/mentee relationship to be effective, both parties have to understand the process – its strengths and its limitations. We suggest that there are some guiding principles – some dos and don'ts – that might help.

In a series of short articles (Watson *et al.*, 1997), Anne Murdoch and Trevor Kerry debated the pros and cons of mentoring. Murdoch played up the positive aspects of mentoring. She noted that the role of mentor in the literature has been subject to many descriptors and images:

- parent figure
- critical friend
- guide
- sponsor
- trainer
- leader
- door opener
- coach
- wise counsellor
- ally
- developer.

She notes the characteristics required of a good mentor and the ways in which such a person must function to be effective. For example, the positive mentor must:

- empathise with the position and role of the mentee
- be willing to give time and listen
- be in a position of sufficient influence to 'make things happen' for the mentee
- have the skill to say when things are not going well and to help to correct them
- be prepared to share his/her own expertise
- understand the distinctions between working and learning.

She, rightly, points out that the success of any mentoring scheme is based on the ability of the mentor and mentee to work together with a shared mutual interest in the work situation that binds them. This work situation must of itself give opportunities for the pair to meet and share time, and it must provide appropriate training for each (for the mentor, on how to exercise the role; and for the mentee, on how to benefit from it). Like other writers, Murdoch is aware that a mentor must have 'credibility', that is, he or she must have been and still be a successful practitioner.

To this catalogue of pre-conditions for success, Kerry added:

- mentors must know how to aid the learning of adults
- they must be able to observe analytically their mentees at work
- they must be reflective practitioners, able to learn themselves by drawing lessons from work practice
- they must have the skills to be able to feedback their insights to their mentees.

Kerry sees the problems inherent in mentoring in the failures of skill on the part of the mentor; hence the emphasis in this chapter on careful mentor selection. He noted some of these failures, and they may be helpful in pointing up where mentoring is going wrong or has the potential to go wrong:

- poor mentors do not give time. Instead of finding well-planned opportunities for mentor sessions, in a quiet place, where confidentiality can be sustained, they try to have hasty, informentee's performance unless some time has been spent in observing it, and in going over evidence (such as documents produced or records kept) of those parts not observed;
- poor mentors do not do their homework. A mentor cannot comment on a mentee's performance unless some time has been spent in observing it, and in going over evidence (such as documents produced or records kept) of those parts not observed;

- poor mentors fail to understand the purpose of mentoring: that it is a process of reflective learning from experience. They treat it at the 'shoulder to cry on' end of the one-to-one continuum rather than at a professional level of radical analysis of situations to extract better performance in the future;

- poor mentors do not give advice or have no guidance to give;

- poor mentors do not follow up on the learning to see what progress has been made;

- poor mentors do not have a genuine interest in, and empathy with, the mentee. (This is often due to poor selection in the first instance.)

Some of the conflict about the value of the mentoring process stems from the philosophies that underlie the concept. If one regards the processes of teaching and of management in education as a craft, then the mentor is the master craftsperson and the process of mentoring is an apprenticeship. All the mentee has to do is to follow in the mentor's footsteps until he or she becomes almost as good as the mentor through a process of imitation.

While we accept that there is a value in imitation (i.e. one can gain some improvement in one's performance as a deputy from modelling oneself on an excellent deputy of one's acquaintance), this is a limited concept. We prefer the 'reflective practitioner' model, which suggests that real learning is gained through having experiences, analysing them – including one's own strengths and weaknesses in the situation – and then using the experiences to formulate a new insight and way of behaving. This is a genuine learning process as opposed to mere imitation. The mentor is the person who has the analytical and reflective skills to guide you in that process of learning.

As a newly appointed or newish deputy, there is a good chance that you will be asked to accept or choose a mentor. The mentoring process may be quite formative in your future career. The choice has to be a good one. Task 29 asks you to think about who you might like as a mentor, and to make this judgement against some criteria that have been established in this chapter.

TASK 29

Selecting a mentor

Use the pro forma that follows as a checklist against which to assess the suitability of a potential mentor

Quality	Your assessment
Has experience of the role	

Has 'credibility'

Can give time

Is an acute observer

Has analytical skills

Can draw out reflective insights

Articulates practice well

Has a calm personality

Makes wise judgements

Has skills as an educator of adults/peers

Of course, as a deputy the tables may well be turned. You are almost certain to find yourself the mentor as well as the mentee. Whom will you mentor? Many deputies we have spoken to are asked to mentor students in training and newly qualified teachers. They may also be called on to mentor non-teaching staff such as specialist teacher assistants.

As a mentor, you will need to exhibit all the characteristics, and demonstrate all the skills, that we have covered in this chapter. How well will you cope? Repeat Task 29 by using the qualities listed to assess your own skills as a potential mentor of new recruits to the profession. Be honest. How well did you do?

Appraisal

Appraisal is a role related to, but different from, mentoring in which a deputy is almost certain to be involved. What are the differences between mentoring and appraisal?

The first difference is that, while schools are not required to put in place schemes of mentoring to support their staff, they are required to set up an appraisal scheme. In most schools the system in place allows for an appraisal once every year or two years. There may well be very specific procedures laid down in the school or by the Local Education Authority. Therefore an early task will be for the deputy to learn the local requirements for appraisal.

TASK 30

Discovering the detail of your school's appraisal scheme

Your school's staff handbook ought to contain details of its appraisal system.

Read up the detail of the scheme before continuing this chapter.

Another significant difference is that appraisal contains an element of judgement, and follow-up is more systematic than in the mentoring process. Appraisal has been defined as:

> *The process whereby an employee and his or her superordinate meet to discuss the work performance of the employee.*
>
> (Fidler and Cooper, 1987)

Appraisal is a kind of 'mentoring with teeth', that looks in partnership at the appraisee's progress and even provides some support through training to meet identified needs, but that is designed specifically to raise standards through proven levels of performance. The key word here is accountability. Nevertheless, many of the features of an appraisal process mirror those of mentoring; and the skills of the appraiser are similar to those of the mentor. Appraisees, like mentees, need to prepare for the process.

It seems reasonable to suggest that appraisers should approach their task using the same skills as mentors, as indicated earlier in the chapter. There is the same need for careful preparation, observation, analysis, reflection and discussion. In fact, the appraiser should:

- assist the appraisee to reflect on performance
- acknowledge achievement
- help to resolve blockages to, and with, progress
- encourage and facilitate improvement.

The appraisal will normally take place at a specified time. The appraisee will probably have been observed at work. The appraisee will have been invited to submit a folio of evidence of work, including their own assessment of their level of performance and any achievements and progress made since the last appraisal. The location should be neutral ground (but in a professional location, not the local pub or the appraiser's home). The location is best if comfortable (with perhaps armchairs and a table to rest papers on), but the appraiser should be wary of pulling rank by sitting behind a big desk on a high chair. The appraisee should be put at ease, as far as possible. Strict confidentiality should be observed. The guidelines of the local scheme on written records and recording of outcomes should be followed strictly.

Appraisal should end with two important outcomes. The first relates to target setting, the second to a strategy for helping the appraisee reach the targets.

Targets in appraisal

The purpose of appraisal is to raise performance. Performance can be raised from whatever baseline: an outstanding teacher can get better, and there is always something that each of us could refine within our repertoire of skills. Therefore, the appraisal needs to generate a set of targets towards this improvement process. Guidelines for this might include that the identified targets following appraisal should be:

- clear and unambiguous
- not too many (say, three to five) so they are not daunting
- clearly measurable: the appraisee must know how success will be determined
- challenging ... but
- realistic and attainable
- job related, so that the gains in the appraisee's competence can be appreciated
- related to the school's mission and vision
- written down, so that both appraisee and appraiser can refresh their memories and there is no dispute
- related to an overall action plan for the appraisee
- monitored and discussed periodically between formal appraisals.

If the targets are well formulated this will aid the second outcome of appraisal.

Training and support

Improvement does not happen because the appraiser demands it or because the appraisee desires it. There must be a means for bringing improvement about. The teacher who is deemed to need improved class-control skills may require the support and mentoring of an experienced colleague. A keen individual teaching a new section of the curriculum may need some time to gain increased subject knowledge. A deputy who is learning the skills of management may be superb at administration, but may benefit from a course on time management.

Appraisal provides a systematic opportunity for the school to target some of its training grant moneys at well-focused professional development.

The place of appraisal in the development of the school

Appraisal fits well within the rationale for school improvement suggested in this book. We have emphasised that each member of staff (teaching or non-teaching) has to take responsibility for the quality of the school as a whole. Appraisal provides a route through which each staff member can render account for their part in that process. It allows the appraiser to assess whether the appraisee has understood, and is working in harmony with, the school's mission and vision. It helps to maximise the human resources of the school: for example, appraisal may throw up hidden strengths of individuals that could be better used. It supports the view of teaching suggested here and of teachers as reflective practitioners.

Just as with mentoring, before leaving appraisal it is necessary to point out that the deputy may well find the tables turned from time to time. He or she will be subject to appraisal, as well as acting as appraiser. The insights gained from appraising may be helpful in this process; but the chances are that it will also work the other way. After all, a deputy is not immune from the insecurities and doubts that dog colleagues on the teaching staff. This two-way process assists empathy and should itself be a factor in performing better as a manager.

Conclusion

Mentoring and appraisal thus share some characteristics; and mentors and appraisers share some skills. The two processes are not identical, and it is important to acknowledge and make clear the differences between them. A similar set of skills relates to a third area of operation identified in this chapter, interviewing. As we shall see, while interviewing (for example, interviewing potential teaching and non-teaching staff for posts) overlaps with mentoring and appraising, it also has a unique set of skills and procedures.

Interviews and interviewing

As a deputy you will almost certainly take some part in interviewing. In a primary school this may be a major role in the appointment of support staff, for example; or in a secondary school perhaps a support role in appointing teaching staff. Certainly, as a deputy the likelihood is that you will not be required to deal with all the processes, such as advertising posts, leading up to the time when an interview takes place. Nevertheless, it would do no harm for you to be aware of some of the pitfalls of these preliminary processes.

An important consideration is the information about the school that is provided to each candidate before application is made. You will recall what has been said in this book about generating a vision for the school and creating a good image. A pack for candidates that includes a scruffy information sheet (as opposed to a pleasant and informative brochure), no map, no indication of the likely interview date, and omits to mention specific material information about the area relating to the post advertised, will not impress good candidates or encourage them to apply.

Usually, each candidate will be asked to complete a standard application form. Each may have written a letter or made a written statement about their candidacy: why they feel they are able to undertake the role advertised. All the applications should be sifted at a short-listing meeting. After short-listing, references are taken up. Two references will have been requested and these should be taken up *before* the interview for all short-listed candidates. All of the information about short-listed candidates should have been copied to the interviewing panel (but to no one else) before the interview. After the interviews, all except one set of papers about the candidates should be collected by the chair and destroyed.

Where institutions and governing bodies can go seriously wrong is in contravening legislation, particularly legislation about equal opportunities and unfair discrimination. This is a topic for a more technical book and will not be dealt with at length here. However, it is worth pointing out the commonest pitfalls:

- normally, it is imperative to advertise posts, not simply to 'appoint from within' without competition;
- each post needs a job description and person specification; judgement about the 'best candidate' has to be against the criteria stated. For example, you cannot advertise for a primary teacher with 'ability to teach music essential' and then appoint someone who does not fulfil the criterion when other candidates do!;
- the same criteria apply to short-listing before interview as to the interviews on the day;
- all candidates must be treated in the same way: if one is offered a tour of the school then all have to be offered one;
- it is not permissible to discriminate on grounds of race, gender or disability except in certain specific circumstances identified in legislation;
- it is not permissible to ask discriminatory questions such as: what will you do if your husband gets a job in another part of the country?

Before the interviews the interviewing panel will have agreed a programme for the candidates: a tour of the school, a talk with key staff, and a timetable for the interviews, for example. When the candidates arrive they should be welcomed, given somewhere to sit out of public view, be provided with some refreshment, be directed to the location of toilets, be given a programme for the session, and be met briefly by the chair of the interviewing panel. Best practice is to encourage candidates to talk freely about the job, to put them at ease, and to assure them that they are choosing the school as much as the school may be choosing them.

All of these processes should be standard practice: it may fall to a deputy to organise some or all of them, though our emphasis here is really with the interviewing procedure, to which we now move.

Let us assume that you are taking part in the interview itself. First, the chair should establish before the interview an area of questioning for each panel member: one may ask about the candidate's educational background, another about teaching experience to date, another about the candidate's ambitions in teaching, and so on. When you have your area of questioning you need to think of one or two questions.

It is surprising how difficult some people find it to ask good questions. Here are some pitfalls to avoid:

- don't ask closed questions that lead to monosyllabic answers, or semi-rhetorical questions: *So you trained in Durham, then?*

- don't lead the candidate: *You would use an overhead projector if it were available, would you?*

- don't ask multiple questions and fail to pause for answers: *What happened to you on your MA course? Was it well taught? What do you think it taught you? Are you intending to go on from there?*

- avoid most hypothetical questions: *What would you do if a student stood up and ...?*

The questions in these examples might have been better if they had been formulated like this:

- what do you think were the strengths of your training course in Durham?

- what audiovisual methods do you find help your teaching?

- would you please describe your MA course?

- to what extent do you think that the course was itself taught in a way that aided your own teaching skills?

- what do you think were the three most important lessons you learned about teaching from this course?

- how do you see your career moving on in, say, the next five years?

- can you describe a situation in which you dealt with a difficult student and say what you did?

While the candidates are answering your questions, and other people's, look interested. You should make eye contact, though you may wish to take notes. We prefer to listen to the answers to our own questions and make notes during the answers to those of other panel members. All the questions should be pithy and brief: the panel needs to give the candidates the floor for most of the interview. Each candidate should have an equal time with the panel. It is the chair's job to keep time. Towards the end of the interview, anything that is unclear should be clarified, and the candidate given a chance to ask their own questions – though not so many as to run over time.

When all the interviews are completed, the chair should gather the panel for a systematic discussion of each candidate. Ideally, this discussion should be closely focused on the criteria for the post and each candidate's suitability. It should not degenerate into personal comment about candidates. Heads and deputies may occasionally have to educate the minority of governors who do not understand the rules of interviewing and appointment on this kind of issue.

When a decision has been made, it is normal for the chair to meet the successful candidate to tie up the formalities of acceptance. Either the chair or members of the panel may be asked to meet unsuccessful candidates to 'debrief' them, i.e. to give some indication of why they were less fitted for the post than the successful person. This must be handled carefully, should be quite a short session, should suggest any areas of weakness (or less strength) and may give one or two hints about future performance (such as 'You might find it useful to attend a course on X' or 'Perhaps it would help you if you were to project Y element of your experience more strongly').

Even here there are potential problems, as one of our deputies found:

> I took part in my first interview panel to appoint a new head of upper school. Everything went really well until after the appointment was made! Then I went back to the staffroom. The internal candidate was there. She was very angry not to have been appointed and challenged me about the issue. I said that it wasn't my decision alone and that the appointment had been made with what the panel believed was the best long-term interest of the school at heart. She even conceded that this was so, but indicated that she had been promised the job some time ago by a member of the panel. Some other staff who had overheard this exchange indicated in private that this was indeed true, but suggested I should not feel guilty since it was not a legitimate thing to do.

Summary

You will have noted that, though the skills of mentoring, appraising and interviewing are different skills, they share some fundamental characteristics. They all depend on interpersonal skills in the lead individual: the ability to put the mentee, appraisee or interviewee at ease, the ability to listen, to question, to establish empathy, to analyse, to reflect and to make judgements. These are all management skills of a high order, that each manager can continue to refine throughout his or her career. They are useful background skills for the next topic in this book: the skill of acting as chair.

Our intention is that, at the end of this chapter, you will have:

- considered the roles of mentor and mentee
- prepared your thoughts in order to choose an effective mentor for yourself
- thought about your skills in mentoring others
- distinguished between mentoring and appraisal
- reflected on the skills of being an effective appraiser
- taken a first look at interviewing for staff appointments.

Chairing skills

B eing a chair is like conducting an orchestra. You are at the heart of a process that is being carried on by others. Yet the tone of the situation, the nature of the debate, the direction of travel, the pace of the proceedings and the quality of the final outcomes all depend on you.

As a deputy, you will be called on to chair a number of groups of varying kinds – some will be informal working parties and some formal committees, or subcommittees that report elsewhere. The same basic skills of chairing and principles of proceeding apply in all cases, though you will have to make judgements about the degree of formality that you choose to operate in each set of circumstances, and according to the nature of the committee.

This chapter aims to give you basic skills that you need in order to be efficient and to start being effective. However, it may help you first to think about badly run meetings that you have attended, using Task 31.

Different chairs have different ways of proceeding, and you will develop your own style. The suggestions we offer here are those we favour, but you may evolve better ones or be able to adapt these into other formats. We shall use the gender-free title 'chair' despite its impersonal tone, simply for convenience.

TASK 31

Recalling your worst ever meeting

Most of us have attended a myriad of meetings in our professional careers. This Task asks you to think back to the worst meeting you ever attended. Try to recall what was wrong with it.

There are a few headings to start off your analysis, but you will need to add to these:

Arrangements

Agenda

Chair's control

Quality of contributions

Decision making

Time keeping

Other:

1

2

3

The order and procedure of meetings

Groundrules 1   Before the meeting

Meetings are best when everyone is clear about how they operate, and when they operate in an orderly fashion. Some meetings (such as subcommittees of governing bodies) have fixed rules on some of the matters discussed here and you need to discover what these are. Others do not, and you can set your own.

There are some key issues that apply to almost every meeting. First, a productive meeting cannot take place unless the members receive an agenda (*see* below) and any briefing papers well in advance – at least one week. But receiving papers is of no value in itself. The chair has to establish a culture in which the members are disciplined enough to read the papers before coming to the meeting. The agenda will set a place and time for the meeting; any other essential information, such as maps and car-parking instructions, should be included where meetings involve those outside the school.

Time is an important issue in most people's lives, so meetings should have *both* a start time and an end time. Meetings of over two hours' duration are unlikely to be productive. It may be opportune to run for three hours if members have to travel a very long way (say, over 100 miles – not ten minutes down the road) to attend. This kind of meeting will be exceptional in school; and even then, concentration spans will wilt and die after three hours.

Make sure in advance that you know who is going to act as clerk to the meeting: it may be a school administrative officer, or it may be a volunteer member. Do not contemplate being both chair and secretary!

Groundrules 2   Constructing an agenda

Agendas have a standard format. However, the way you put the agenda together – particularly the main business sections – will condition how efficient the meeting is at dealing with the important and urgent business. The standard order is:

- welcome, introductions and apologies
- minutes of the previous meeting
- matters arising from the minutes of the previous meeting
- correspondence (if any)
- reports (if any)
- motions, resolutions and matters for discussion [the main business]
- any other business (AOB)
- date, time and place of the next meeting.

In constructing the agenda, you need to bear in mind the advice given below about moving through the early parts of the agenda quickly, then ordering the main items so that they are dealt with in a logical order – the outcomes of one item may influence another, for example – and in an order that reflects importance and urgency.

The chair has a right to decide what goes on the agenda, but would be foolish not to include items that were important to members. There should always be an opportunity for members to contribute items. This may be an open invitation to submit items to the chair (or the secretary/clerk if there is a regular post holder). Or it may be that an invitation is sent out before each meeting. Either way, items must usually be received two weeks before the next meeting to allow for them to be written into the agenda and the agenda to be circulated a week in advance of the meeting (*see* above).

Groundrules 3   During the meeting

Meetings should run to quite tight rules of procedure. Some meetings are bound by specific sets of procedures that are written down. If this is the case with the meeting you are chairing, make sure that you read the rules and procedures and operate them. In all meetings people should behave in standard ways:

- they address the chair, not each other
- they speak one at a time

- they maintain good order and discipline
- they stick to the agenda and its order
- they behave within any rules governing the meeting, e.g. they do not introduce major items of business under any other business (*see* below) if this is precluded in the rules.

It is the chair's task to ensure that members stick to the rules. Where several members are anxious to speak, for example, the chair will indicate the order in which they are to contribute.

Groundrules 4   After the meeting

The records of meetings are called minutes, and they are useful in keeping members (especially anyone unavoidably absent for a meeting) in touch and up to date with the business of the committee. To be of value they have to be prepared and circulated soon after the meeting. The practice of sending out minutes of the last meeting with the agenda for the next is really rather sloppy. Members can be encouraged, if necessary, to keep a meetings file with all the minutes in and to bring it to each meeting. Providing an attractive file may go some way to assisting this in the more important committees.

In addition, any correspondence generated by the meeting should be attended to straight after the meeting.

Starting off

Meetings start with welcome, introductions and apologies. Of these, the last is the most formal. But it is good practice for the chair to welcome members, even if they are all known colleagues. Anyone new to the meeting should be made to feel welcome by being introduced, so that their presence is not a mystery. Also, in most committees, only members should be present, so the presence of any unknown person should be explained. Occasionally individuals (such as foreign educationists visiting schools) are invited as observers, but the permission of members for the person to remain should be sought – and if any controversial or confidential business arises, the observer should be asked to leave the room for the duration of the item.

Apologies may have been communicated in writing in advance; ask those present whether there are any other apologies for absence.

Minutes of the previous meeting

The next item on the agenda will be the minutes of the previous meeting. Members should have read these. They should be moved and seconded by members as a correct record, and signed by the chair. If there are amendments of accuracy (and only of accuracy), these can be incorporated at this stage.

Matters arising

Next comes matters arising, i.e. any issues from the previous minutes that need further reporting or discussion. Under this agenda item there should be strict limits to the time spent. The most efficient way to handle this is for the chair:

- to limit discussion to items not otherwise on the current agenda
- to invite any formal reports or updates on items listed on the minutes in the order in which they appear on the minutes
- to accept any other matters arising.

Sometimes the chair will go through each item asking for any further comment, or if the minutes are long the chair may go page by page in the same way. The pitfall to avoid is spending a significant time revisiting the business of the last meeting and not getting on with the fresh agenda.

Correspondence

There may be correspondence generated by the previous meeting and the clerk may be asked to report back on this. On the other hand, this business may have been covered incidentally under matters arising.

Reports

If part of the task of the meeting is to receive reports from other committees or working groups, then these appear next on the agenda. The chair should invite the relevant representative of the subgroup to present the report and will then invite discussion or decisions. The chair should thank the presenter.

Other major business

The rest of the agenda will contain the remaining items for discussion by the committee. These items are often the most important ones on the agenda, so it is vital to move on the early parts of the meeting so that time can be given to these discussions. As indicated above, the chair will have prioritised these items. So if the meeting runs out of time and items have to be deferred, it will be those that rate lowest in importance or urgency that are left over.

At the end of each item it may be necessary to make a decision. One member should propose and another second a motion on the issue: a vote can be taken or an agreement reached by a general 'aye'. The chair may propose a motion but still needs a seconder.

Any other business (AOB)

There are professional meetings manipulators who use this item to introduce key items for decision, just when members are running out of energy and the debate is beginning to flag. The danger is that people may be anxious to move on to another commitment and will pass a motion or skimp discussion simply to get the meeting over. This is where a chair has to be strong and set up the groundrule that only quick and relatively trivial items are dealt with under this heading, e.g. points of information. A chair can stipulate that substantive items are brought to the next agenda as full agenda items, and placed high on the agenda so that they are accorded full discussion. The message here is: be firm.

Date, time and place of the next meeting

This sounds innocuous, but it can develop into half an hour of comparative diary watching. Avoid this. If meetings operate on a regular cycle, at a regular time and place, then decisions should be simpler. The only real issue should be, for example, to move the meeting by a week if the regular date happens to be a Bank Holiday or a special event. As a last resort, and if the date cannot be speedily agreed, close the discussion and say that members will be contacted individually for their availability. Then you can send round a response sheet with alternatives, and the date with the highest number of members available wins!

 Helpful hints for chairs

Now that we have looked at the procedures for meetings and at some ways in which they can be made to run more smoothly and efficiently, the task of this section is to examine in a little more detail the skills of chairing.

Chairing meetings well looks easy, but is actually quite a difficult skill to master. Perhaps the first role for the chair is to do the necessary homework: read all the papers, scrutinise the agenda, and think through what might emerge as the sticking points. It is also useful to have a notional timescale in your mind, e.g. you may identify the most important item and decide that you need to make sure there are 45 minutes of debating time for it. In other words, try to develop a plan of the meeting before it takes place. Your plan won't always mirror reality, but it often will.

Always start the meeting on time, even if people are still arriving or pouring the coffee: they will quickly realise that you mean to be businesslike and will conform and function accordingly. Move through the early parts of the agenda quickly, as described above. A good clerk will help by having apologies, correspondence and so on at their fingertips. Assume that everyone has read all the papers. Sometimes it will be necessary to table a late paper; be generally discouraging of this. If an important late paper does have to be tabled, then pause the meeting and give people time to read it. As soon as a few people have finished and there is a suggestion of conversation, move on!

Allow full and open discussion of issues. Don't let one or two powerful individuals dominate; bring out the reluctant contributors. Table 12.1 sets out some useful skills for chairs.

TABLE 12.1 Some useful skills for chairs

- make sure the room and furniture are set out appropriately and are adequate for the purpose, and the room is warm enough or ventilated

- make eye contact

- encourage contributions (e.g. by asking non-contributors if they wish to add any points to those already made) – but don't pressurise

- use supportive comments to an infrequent contributor, e.g. 'Thank you for that contribution; that's a useful point we had missed'

- keep discussion moving by asking pertinent questions

- as chair, your own contributions should normally be very brief. If you want to make a significant contribution to a debate, or have a personal interest in an issue, you should stand down from the chair for that section of the meeting

- keep contributors relevant and on task

- keep the discussion to your notional timescale except in unusual circumstances

- try to draw each discussion towards a conclusion and, where needed, a decision

- use minutes to record decisions at each meeting; and do not allow old debates to be re-opened at the next meeting

- learn when to make the judgement *not* to bring things to a decision: you can always defer a decision to another meeting, set up an interim working group, gather more information, get expert advice from someone who is not a member of the committee, and so on

- if the discussion is a long one, summarise where the debate is going from time to time

- at the end of a discussion, reflect back to the members where you think the debate has reached

- if an issue goes to a vote, record the numbers for, against and abstaining

- an issue is carried unanimously if a show of hands gives everyone voting in favour

- an issue is carried *nem con* if, when the chair asks for an expression of opinion, there is a general 'aye' with no one registering a contrary view

- if a debate has been protracted, check with the clerk that the decisions have been minuted correctly before moving on

Despite your very best efforts, some meetings will be more successful than others. This partly depends on the 'chemistry' you engender in the group. It may be appropriate for some meetings to be less formal, for example, and to be used to explore issues where no decisions are made. A parents' group might give up a meeting to learning some aspect of their children's curriculum, for instance. Such activities can build team spirit and a sense of identity in the group. Some meetings, by contrast, may involve local politicians who are reluctant to depart from set-piece points in opposition to one another. You will have to work harder to break down this kind of barrier.

In-house committees in school can also take a variety of formats and may exhibit similar features. This is often because some people are 'political animals'. The next section looks at some ways of recognising the symptoms of this problem and makes some suggestions for dealing with it.

———— Members' ploys ————

Committees and other similar groups wield power. It is therefore inevitable that individuals will try to manipulate what committees do and what they decide to suit their personal preconceptions and advantages. This section looks at some of the ploys that members use to gain advantage. As you become more experienced as a chair, you may discover others.

The metaphor we have used to describe this is that of 'the political animal'. We did not invent the metaphor; it has a long history in the English language. Back in the 1980s the Industrial Society used the idea in its training programmes. It produced a picture of a group of teachers seated around a committee table at a staff meeting, except that each person's head had been replaced by the head of an animal that epitomised the individual's characteristics. From memory, the commentary went a bit like this:

- the giraffe: too lofty to become involved in the business of the meeting
- the monkey: actively minding other people's business
- the shire horse: faithfully allowing jobs to be offloaded on to him/her
- the lion: roaring a lot but signifying very little.

By now you have probably got the idea. More recently we revived this metaphor, but have tried to invent slightly more subtle (in some cases!) images:

- the hedgehog: hard to get to grips with; retreats into protective covering every time there's a problem
- the butterfly: good public image, but not much substance
- the owl: wise, aloof, still working when everyone else has gone home
- the stork: elevated approach, but with a nasty habit of dumping unwanted packages on you
- the gun dog: soft mouth, loves to be loved
- the tiger: dangerous and unpredictable; manages in bite-size chunks.

Now you have grasped the concept, you might try Task 32.

TASK 32

Inventing your own committee 'animals'

First, try putting some characteristics to these:

- the snake (in the grass)
- the bush baby
- the rabbit
- the unicorn.

Then, invent a few animals of your own along with their peculiar qualities! (This is best done by observing real committees at work.)

1

2

3

Of course, this is just a bit of fun – though there is a remarkable degree of truth in it.

But there are some specific ploys that 'meetings buffs' use to manipulate proceedings:

- some members use the rules of the meeting effectively – if a debate is moving in the 'wrong' direction for them, they find procedural reasons for the proposed actions being out of line with the rules

- some members talk for so long that nothing gets done, which is called filibustering

- some members form alliances outside the meeting to control the direction of debates and the voting

- some members will make proposals to interrupt the flow of a debate that looks set to go against them, e.g. 'We have been in session a long time, I move that we defer a decision until the next meeting'

- some members are 'nitpickers', spending forever on getting every last detail of the minutes into precisely the right phrasing (so make sure the minutes are sound before the meeting!) – they often just waste time, though 'nitpicking' can be a useful skill in the final planning stages of a project

- some members become fixated on the previous meeting, feeling more comfortable with the matters arising than with new business

- some members don't read papers or inform themselves sufficiently, and can divert an otherwise good discussion through irrelevant contributions

- some members defend the status quo at any cost with any one of a thousand variations on the themes:
  - we have done it before (and it didn't work then)
  - we don't have the resources
  - the head won't like it
  - it's against union rules, and so on.

Part of the joy and excitement of running good meetings is to recognise the political animals and the ploys of the meeting-buffs and to be able to counter them, keeping the meeting on task and productive. It is a rare skill and one to which you would do well to pay detailed attention.

———— Summary ————

Our intention is that, at the end of this chapter, you will have:

- understood factors that make meetings productive or unproductive
- become familiar with procedures for meetings
- improved your skills as a chairperson
- developed some strategies to prevent the purpose of meetings being subverted by 'political animals'.

Planning, reporting and public speaking

This chapter aims to help you improve your performance in some important areas of communication. It is about increasing your personal confidence, as well as being about 'getting the message across'. This message is related to the vision, mission and values that you help propagate for your school. But James Champy warns:

> *With values, however, there is a strict limit to the usefulness of purely verbal communications. We must also communicate by acts. If we don't we will create the worst, and possibly the most common of all destructive corporate cultures – a culture of hypocrisy and cynicism. The verbal must be backed up by the actual; words must be followed by deeds.*
>
> (Champy, 1995, p. 91)

Champy goes on to look at the kinds of people who are employable in the successful enterprises of the present and the future. He lists their characteristics (based on Champy, 1995, pp. 157–8):

- they must be able to communicate, to be clear about what they want and need
- they must be persuasive, even eloquent in team, service and mentoring situations
- they must be able to make relationships and handle people sensitively
- they must be self-confident, able to take initiatives and take decisions
- they must know how to respond to change
- they must listen, win authority and lead.

The three topics that are covered in this chapter will give you some of the skills you need to build up your confidence and to lead effectively, but they will also help to improve your ability to put across, and act out, the message that you want to convey. The skills discussed here will be invaluable both on the job and during interviews for more senior education posts.

Planning: the background

In a school context, a great deal of planning will relate to the kinds of matters that find their ways into school development planning. This planning takes place, however, within the wider context of the school's vision and mission. The planning process operates at two levels, therefore:

- at the level of the strategic intent – that is, the broad view about 'where we want to be' and the strategies that are put in place as steps along the road to that goal
- at the level of the day-to-day development planning, in which the nuts and bolts of the school's plant, finances, curriculum and staffing are developed.

We do not see these two processes as contradictory. The strategic intent drives the immediate planning process. We have discussed vision and mission elsewhere in the book, so here the emphasis is on short-term planning – the sort of planning that delivers a revised curriculum in science, or improves student behaviour, or delivers a better school brochure. This is the kind of planning that a deputy will be concerned with on a daily basis, and about which it is also likely that the deputy will be required to report to staff and governors at various times.

The planning process: an overview

You have been given a job to do, a project to complete within the overall mission to the school. What are the steps you will need to go through? Who will you need to involve? How will you carry others with you? How do you deal with accountability for delivering on this task?

In this section we pick up the theme of improving the school brochure, previously examined in Chapter 10 as part of dealing with external relations, but we focus here specifically on the planning process itself as part of that overall task.

Stage 1   Clarifying the intentions

Whatever the task, the first stage is always to define precisely what it is that you are trying to achieve. If you are leading a team to carry out the task, it is still important for you to clarify your own thinking first. It is useful to commit your plan to paper, but at this stage it can be just a rough outline, even a diagram, for your own eyes only.

If you can't formulate what you are trying to achieve in a series of half a dozen bullet points, with maybe some indications of sequence, then you will not begin to convince others. These bullet points are intentions, not outcomes or even means to an end. Intentions are like 'visions': they set out where you want to be, the destination.

Stage 2   Deciding on the personnel

The next job is to decide who is going to help take you to this destination, to build the team. Many plans need to involve key 'others' who will help to implement them. For example, to improve your school brochure you will need people with keyboarding skills, with a good eye for a picture, with a mind for detail (to scrutinise the text for errors), with a feel for marketing, and so on.

Earlier we discussed team roles. Some people provide creativity, some deliver a lot of work, and some are experts on specific issues. Getting the composition and balance right is important. Some of the team will be teaching staff, some non-teachers. You may use outside experts (someone you pay as a consultant or photographer, for example), or you may have people on your governing body or in the PTA who will act in these roles.

In any event, what is important is for the team to be focused on the task. Avoid the 'stone age obstructionists' and 'been there, seen it, done it and it didn't work' brigade. Think about bringing in at least one person who may have little to contribute except enthusiasm now, but who is willing to learn and take a lead in the future.

Stage 3   Articulating the plan

This is the stage at which you outline your ideas to the team. They need to know the intentions – what they have to achieve. But they will have some ideas of their own about how to embark on the journey. Listen. In a team not all the good ideas have to come from you! One manager we knew used to say:

> *This institution is a club. The membership fee is one idea.*

This is a useful concept. At the end of this discussion you need to emerge with a set of intentions that can be translated into intermediate actions towards the goal and that can be ordered in regard to timescale. Responsibilities also need to be allocated.

You now have a schema for action, with intermediate targets and target dates. This is the time to set the whole plan out on paper and to distribute it to the team so that everyone knows who is doing what by when.

Stage 4   Putting the plan into action

Once the plan is finalised, the team members can go away and get their individual jobs done. Your role now is to co-ordinate, to encourage, and to check that things are going according to plan. If they are not, this is the moment to intervene. If there is an impasse of some kind, talk to the appropriate team member and formulate an alternative route to achieve the desired end.

It will be crucial to hold short meetings during this time so that everyone can be briefed about progress. It also encourages team members not to become stalled – the team depends on them! Make meetings short, pithy and task oriented; they are an opportunity to refocus on the intentions.

Stage 5   Moving to completion

'A promise is only a promise until it is delivered' goes the slogan. Your plan has to become a reality for it to have validity and value. So the individual members have to carry out their tasks, and the co-ordinator has to orchestrate them into a synthesis, and the final decisions and actions have to be taken. In the present case, the new school brochure has to be completed, printed and delivered – and it has to have achieved its intentions! Completion then involves evaluation and an assessment of lessons learned. Too often this very last stage is forgotten.

Summary

Planning is a tool. It helps the leader or manager focus on the issues that need to be tackled in order to complete a task or project. Knowing the processes in planning, and thinking about them systematically, helps. Of course, every situation is slightly different from any other; any planning process is unique in that sense.

Table 13.1 uses the problem discussed here – planning a new school brochure – to illustrate some of the points made above. Look at this before you move on to the next section of this chapter, which helps you think about how you report on a project or talk to those to whom you are accountable: the head, the governors or a committee.

| TABLE 13. 1 | A project planning outline |

Project:	To improve the school brochure
Intentions:	1 To provide a brochure that will attract the attention of the client audience
	2 To make the brochure user friendly
	3 To improve the brochure's visual impact
	4 To produce the brochure by 30 September

The team:	John	Social scientist and member of PTA
	Me	SMT member and responsible for 'legwork'
	Secretary	To provide keyboarding skills, good liaison with potential clients
	Mary	Good at design and colour
	Simon	Has a good flair for language and clear expression
	Hilary	A nitpicker, will eliminate errors, and be interested to get more involved next year

The plan:

Task	Who does it?	By what date?
Undertake market research on present brochure to establish its strengths and weaknesses	John	15 April
Team meeting to discuss findings	Me	22 April
Research improved layout of type	Secretary	21 May
Research possible photographers	Mary	21 May
Work over the content for user-friendly language	Simon	21 May
Check statutory content	Me	21 May
Team meeting to report back	Me	28 May
Make key decisions ready for mock-up phase		
Following decisions, to mock up new content	Simon and Hilary	20 June
Provide sample layouts	Secretary	20 June
Book the photographer	Mary	3 June
Get photos taken	Mary	20 June

Get quotes	Me	1 July
Team meeting: putting it all together	Me	25 July
At this stage we will have a complete draft brochure		
Check outcome with head and make any amendments	Me	30 July
Final brochure stage		
Deal with printer	Me	10 August
Check proofs	Team	7 Sept
End product: Take delivery	Me	21 Sept

―――――― Reporting ――――――

In this section we shall deal with written reporting, since oral reporting will be covered in the final section on public speaking.

One of the common tasks of managers is to present reports to committees. For a deputy head this will usually mean to a group of colleagues on the staff or to the governing body.

Reporting in writing is not a difficult task to master, yet many people fail to do it well. This is most often because they fail to follow some quite straightforward rules. These rules are set out in Table 13.2.

TASK 33 ――――――――――――――――――――――――

Writing a report for committee

Take a topic on which you have to present a report to a group of staff, parents or governors. Write a short report in the light of the advice given in Table 13.2.

Circulate the report before the meeting, for example with the agenda for the meeting. Try to assess whether people read it and what reactions your report received.

Your mentor will also be able to comment on it.

If you receive any negative feedback, take note of the points made so as to avoid problems next time.

TABLE 13.2 Rules for reporting in writing

1 *Keep it simple:* the people to whom you will be reporting are, like you, busy. They want to get straight to the facts. A frequent error in all educational documents is to use complicated words and phrases when simple everyday language would do. But don't talk down to the audience.

2 *Keep it short:* because the readers are busy, say what you have to say in the smallest quantity of words necessary to do justice to the topic.

3 *Avoid jargon and acronyms:* nothing is more irritating than to be presented with a document full of jargon words and phrases that, in truth, signify very little. Acronyms are almost as bad: no one wants to have to stop reading to look up what they mean!

4 *Lay the text out neatly:* a document that is wordprocessed attractively is easier to read than one in too small print, with poor paragraphing and so on. Change the typeface for different sections of text, for example.

5 *Use subheadings:* these should guide the reader through the document. It is a good ploy to have questions as subheadings, with the suggested answers in the following paragraph.

6 *Make use of numbers and bullet points:* lists can be extremely helpful in keeping your message simple and clear.

7 *Draw a conclusion or provide a short summary:* this will guide the readers to your argument, even if they have lost the thread slightly or if it is some time since they read your whole text.

The report shown as Table 13.3 is not meant to be exemplary – it contains good and bad features.

TASK 34

Analysing a written report

Go through the report in Table 13.3 itemising what you see as its strengths and what you see as its weaknesses. After you have completed this Task, you can consult the commentary at the end of the chapter.

What have you learned from this process?

TABLE 13.3 A sample report for analysis

To: All teaching and non-teaching colleagues

From: Deputy Head

Staff meeting 1 May Paper 3

Improving playground behaviour

The problem

Over the last four weeks there have been an increasing number of incidents on the playground involving minor acts of bullying, depositing of litter, and rough play leading to injury. The head and I deemed it necessary to act before either there was a more serious incident or a culture of indiscipline began to become endemic.

Initial action

The senior management team met yesterday and decided on some courses of action that needed to be taken by members of staff at various levels.

The action plan

It was decided:

1 That the *head* and *deputy* would rota themselves to have a presence on the playground at least once during every break and lunchtime.

2 That at break times each *member of staff* on duty should:

- ensure arrival on the playground before the children
- stay on the playground after the break until everyone has left
- be extra vigilant for examples of poor tidiness or bad behaviour
- intervene quickly to stop problems escalating
- use every opportunity to discuss with their own classes the dimensions of good personal behaviour in school and of course outside it.

3 The *head* will run a special assembly on caring for others early next week to reinforce the overall theme. She will explain the LEA-favoured POSIDISC scheme, which of course we subscribe to.

4 At mealtimes, the *lunchtime supervisors* will be supported for part of each session by a member of SMT.

The future

Ultimately the plan will be to provide better training for lunch supervisors and we have contacted Rhombus On-site Training to quote for this. They will take cognisance of our mission statement, and Helen will keep them on track as always.

Meanwhile ...

We want everyone to be extra vigilant on corridors. Thank you.

John Smith

Public speaking

Public speaking requires many of the skills already discussed in this chapter. Whether the deputy is called on to present a short report at a staff meeting or to make a longer presentation to governors or parents, much of the same advice applies. For example, whatever the deputy wants to say must have been well planned in the first instance: it is impossible to put across an idea that is poorly thought through. Second, the thoughts must have been ordered – probably on paper – just as they would for a written presentation. Only at this point is it feasible to think about delivering a good oral presentation.

Having reached this stage, it is possible to give the would-be public speaker some quite firm guidelines on which to proceed, and this we have done with the checklist in Table 13.4.

TABLE 13.4 **Some rules for successful public speaking**

- think of a good, attention-catching way to introduce the topic you are going to talk about. Cast your eyes over the two examples below to get the flavour of this advice:

> *Example 1: Tonight I have been asked to speak to you about the exciting way we teach mathematics in this school. I know most of you will think 'Oh, how boring', but I hope by the time I've finished it won't be.*
>
> *Example 2: I guess that if we conducted a straw poll in the audience this minute about the subject you used to like least when you were all pupils in school the largest proportion would probably nominate maths. In this school, maths is very definitely fun, as our two young volunteers are going to demonstrate ...*

- define any technical terms or concepts you use. This may sound obvious, but as with written presentations it is all too easy to slip in without explanation things like DfEE, SATs, Teacher Training Agency, formative, positive reinforcement

- link anything you say to concrete experience or to real examples with which the audience can relate

- order and sequence the things you want to say in a logical way. Don't leave out steps in an explanation, and be sure that you include everything that the audience needs to know

- think about your use of language. Connectives – but, however, meanwhile, consequently – enhance the meaning of what you say for the audience. Some people really do manage without these, and their presentations become a sequence of unconnected factual statements that lack meaning and significance

- linguistic ploys are also a valuable tool. These are things like pausing, emphasis, repetition. Consider the following examples:

> *Example 1: Your child can opt for any one of the subjects on list A. If he or she wants to study one of those on list B, he/she will have to travel to our other site across the road.*
>
> *Example 2: It may help you if you now look at list A. [Pause] All the subjects on list A are taught in this building here, where you now are. Of course, your child can also choose subjects from list B. However, it is important that you understand that these subjects – and only these subjects – are taught in the building across the road.*

- the pace of the presentation is important: too quick, and people will fail to follow it; too slow, and they will lose the thread of the argument. In both cases the outcome is the same: boredom

- in written presentations you were urged to use numbered points. In spoken ones you can use the same technique to help the audience keep hold of the 'conceptual map' of what you are saying: first we do x, second we do y, then we undertake step z, and finally …

- in a classroom you would look for feedback to check understanding. With a presentation you may consider using the same technique by offering a period for questions at the end.

As well as advice about what to *do*, it may be helpful to have a little advice about what *not* to do with oral explanations.

First, a common mistake is to start with an apology. This often makes the audience cringe ('Unaccustomed as I am to public speaking', or 'I'm sorry to have to bore you with this …' – *and you just did!*).

Second, jokes are something of a bone of contention. The simplest advice is don't start with a joke – if it falls flat you're dead in the water as a presenter. The problem with jokes is that there are so many things you can't make jokes about: politics, religion, sex, and even education. There is always the chance of real misunderstanding, and someone in the audience is bound to take offence whatever the joke, or at best write you off as a trivial person. Save the jokes for your next wedding reception when everyone expects them.

Finally, beware of relying on reams of notes and looking at them non-stop. Try never to use the full text of your talk. You could have headings written boldly on cards, to guide and sequence your talk and give you confidence. Make these cards unobtrusive; for example, use them on a lectern rather than stand in front of an audience thumbing through them openly. (In the latter case, the audience will be counting how many you still have to get through!) Number them, so that if they do get out of sequence you can quickly restore order. Check the room lighting, to make sure that when the audience is assembled you can actually read the cards (some lecture theatres have lights that dim, for example).

Supporting your presentation with audiovisual aids

We have dealt with this as a separate item because it has own peculiar pitfalls, at least for some presenters. Your presentation is likely to be clearer and more professional if you use audiovisual materials to back it up. However, this will only be true if you are familiar with how to operate the technology. For example, it is not uncommon to see speakers whom one would expect to know better fail to work an overhead projector, or try to use transparencies that are poorly handwritten, or typed in too small a font to be visible to the audience.

The same kinds of comments apply to any form of projection. If you need a screen, check the size-to-audience ratio before the presentation. If you use video, know where on the tape the extract is and make sure that the screen is big enough. Know whether the room lights dim and how to operate them. For larger audiences, if you choose to use a sound system, try out your distance from the microphone in advance, and beware of knocking the microphone or of moving around while you speak since this will alter the sound quality. In public speaking, this kind of preparation is everything.

Summary

This chapter has reviewed a cluster of skills that properly belong together because they share a number of characteristics and pitfalls. Whether seeking a deputy headship or, later, a headship, these skills may be what marks you out from others during the kinds of simulation exercises often required at the interview stage as well as being integral to the role itself. But it is worth referring back to Champy's comment at the beginning of this chapter. Words alone are not enough: having established the plans and the rhetoric, it is then necessary to live the message.

Our intention is that, at the end of this chapter, you will have:

- examined critically the planning process (for a school project, for compiling the school development plan)
- analysed the skills of written report writing and practised them
- grasped the main principles of delivering a good oral report (e.g. at a parents' evening).

COMMENTARY ON TASK 34

The report starts quite promisingly: it identifies the audience and the sender. It also has a relevant title, an indication of the date by which it should be read, and it outlines the issue succinctly. It uses headings quite well, as well as numbers and bullet points.

Less positive features include the following:

- type sizes and faces are possibly more disruptive than helpful
- some might discuss whether the issue should have been debated by staff (teaching and non-teaching), not just by the SMT
- the report could be seen as patronising towards lunch supervisors
- who is Helen, and what exactly is she going to do?
- does everyone understand SMT? And POSIDISC (the Authority's positive discipline policy)?
- there are some small errors of grammar
- 'cognisance' approaches jargon
- what precisely is the relationship of 'corridor' problems to the rest of the document's concern for breaktime litter and aggression? There could be one, but it is not explained.

Budgets and finance

Before becoming a deputy, your contact with budgets and finance may have been limited to managing a small departmental budget and to a brief overview of the yearly accounts. As deputy, your role in this process will obviously have to change. Although (in a primary school in particular) you may still have direct control of a particular budget head, linked to other responsibilities, you also need to have an overview of the overall budgeting process and in relation to this will most probably work, at least in a supportive and advisory capacity, with the headteacher.

—— Some theoretical issues ——

Different people and different institutions approach the process of budgeting in rather different ways. In schools you are likely to meet two main approaches, and these tend to sit at either end of a continuum:

Historical budgeting ————— Zero-based budgeting

What does this mean?

In many educational institutions, the allocation of funds exists simply on the basis of 'what departments had last year'. In a secondary setting, once the fixed costs (for things like staff wages, cleaning, electricity, rates etc.) are taken out of the equation, the relatively modest sum remaining will be split between departments. In a primary school there may be fewer 'fund holders': perhaps the head of each Key Stage and the head of nursery. The area of the budget that they control is called a cost centre. In the extreme case of historical budgeting, or incremental budgeting as it is also called, the sums given out annually to each cost centre will be the same as those allocated in previous years, subject to adjustments for inflation or for fluctuations in the size of the overall budget. In an actual situation, therefore, historical budgeting means that if the science department receives three times more than the history department, it will always receive three times more regardless of other circumstances.

By contrast there is ZBB – zero-based budgeting. In an extreme case, ZBB means that every financial year every cost centre, through its fund holder, must argue the case for an allocation of money from scratch. In this case, fund holders would bring to some form of decision-making finance committee proposals for expenditure supported by evidence of need. These would be sifted, their merits discussed, some proposals would be supported and others would be partially funded or would drop out altogether.

Table 14.1 sets out the merits and demerits of these two systems.

TABLE 14.1 Merits and demerits of incremental and zero-based budgeting

Incremental budgeting	Zero-based budgeting
Relies on history	Starts each budget cycle with a clean sheet
Tinkers at the edges	Can promote radical reform
Goes unchanged and unchallenged	May produce conflict and controversy
Limits debate	Opens up debate about priorities
Perpetuates inefficiency	Requires justification
Provides stability	Is time consuming
Fails to provide for initiatives	Allows for initiatives
May lead to spending without careful analysis of need	Means that expenditure is prioritised
Protects the powerful	Defends the weak

Budgeting and management

This book is about management practice, and about practising management more effectively. We need, therefore, to place budgeting within a management context before considering how it might work in a practical situation.

Budgeting is not just about spending money; it is about the management of resources to achieve broader management ends. There is a sequence of events that needs to take place to ensure the effectiveness of using the school's money. Clearly, the management process begins with formulating the overall intentions (the vision, the mission) for the school. This in turn implies an analysis of the organisation and of the staffing to achieve those ends. Plans are put into place. At this point the budget has to be utilised in order to facilitate those plans. Then the money must be spent – the budget is implemented. The results are evaluated and fed back into the next cycle of intentions.

Budgets also have taken on a wider significance since Local Management of Schools came into being and since the Government's more recent Fair Funding initiative. There are clear political intentions that school budgets must be seen (by parents, governors, the wider community) to be well planned, to achieve their aims, to be cost efficient and to be effective in delivering better education (value for money). Indeed, schools – through the inspection process – are held accountable in these areas.

Having established these management principles, we can move on to look at some of the ways in which deputy heads might be involved with the realities of budget organisation.

———— Budgeting: some practical issues ————

In many schools, the overall budget process is designed to last for nearly two years, with four main phases, as shown in Table 14.2.

TABLE 14.2 The budget process

1 Preliminary analysis	Strategic	Before financial year
2 Budget construction	Operational	Before financial year
3 Control and monitoring of expenditure	Operational	During financial year
4 Evaluation	Strategic	After financial year

Source: from Knight, B. (1993) *Financial Management for Schools*, Harlow: Longman.

The processes described in Table 14.2 are interlinked. Obviously, there is strong linkage of processes 1 and 2 for any forthcoming financial year, and process 4 will be heavily linked to processes 1 and 2 for the following year. Therefore, in practice these processes will appear very much as a cycle, rather than discrete activities.

It is important that as well as being aware of the processes of budgeting, you are familiar with the categorisation and layout of budgets. There are three main types in use (line-item, function, programme). The first two are shown in Table 14.3.

The programme format links expenditure more closely to objectives and you would expect to see such headings as subjects in this format, but you may also see very specific headings, such as 'gifted children'. This method is much more difficult to calculate if it is used fully, since such costs as teaching staff and cleaning staff would need to be spread across the programme headings. However, it could usefully be used in conjunction with the other formats to indicate the costs of key development projects, and is definitely likely to be loosely used within School Development Planning.

TABLE 14.3 Budget layouts

Line-item	Function
Employees	Instruction
Full time/part-time teachers	Full-time/part-time teachers
Supply teachers	Supply teachers
Supply teachers (INSET)	Technical
Administrative/clerical	Books and equipment
Technical	Administration
Caretakers	Full-time teachers
Premises	Administrative, clerical
Electricity	Postage and telephone
Water	Premises
Cleaning materials	Caretakers
Refuse collection	Electricity
Maintenance	Water
Supplies and services	Insurance
Books and equipment	Teacher support services
Postage and telephone	INSET
Establishment	Supply teachers (INSET)
Advertising	Clerical support
Staff travel/subsistence	Student support and services
Insurance	Transportation
Miscellaneous	Catering

Source: from Knight (1993)

Some teachers feel that such issues are 'accountants' gobbledygook' and that 'education shouldn't be about economics'. However, one has to accept that although ideology and vision are laudable, they need to operate within the constraints of the 'real world'. Economics and vision should by no means be seen as totally incompatible; indeed, one should support the other and economic reality can sometimes provide opportunities, as well as being a constraint.

As we have seen, the budgeting process is a powerful management tool when used properly. It is certainly, at the very least, an essential element of a school's strategic planning cycle. Government directives strongly commend the linkage of budgeting to the School Development Planning cycle and although central dictates are not always to be welcomed, this one obviously makes logical sense. All too often, when initiatives and ideas are proposed, they are not fully costed. When this happens, the chances of success are severely reduced. Most initiatives not only require additional resourcing, but usually take up a great deal of time, and time often appears to be the rarest and most valuable commodity of all in education nowadays. Time is, in a literal sense, money.

In the following case study, a deputy reflects on how an initiative, led by her, was enhanced by its linkage to the budgetary process.

CASE STUDY

Time really is money

All too often, as a deputy, I find myself having to cram 101 jobs into my 'spare time' (whatever that is!). I expect this as part of the role, but if a development is really important, then just trying to fit it in isn't always the best option. Recently, I was leading an initiative to develop our school pupil tracking system. This was allocated a specific budgetary amount in the SDP of £300 – this doesn't sound much, but it certainly had an impact.

The resource implications were relatively low, the software package chosen to support it cost just £80, but the main issue was going to be time. Key activities that were necessary to ensure successful development were:

1. Looking at our current range of records of pupil achievement.

2. Researching alternative systems.

3. Seeking LEA advice.

4. Visiting one or two other schools who have already established systems.

5. Consulting/liaising with staff and head on the strengths and weaknesses of alternative decisions.

6. Familiarisation, implementation, monitoring and evaluation of chosen system (includes checking pro formas are being correctly used; entering of data into computer; generation, interpretation and evaluation of comparative data).

Although activity 6 is only just beginning and the budget allocation is almost spent, I am now confident and happy with integrating the on-going maintenance of the scheme within my regular duties. The time needed to carry out activities 1–5 was not fully covered by the £220 available, which allowed for two days' supply cover. I still used some of my own time. However, if there had not been the allocation to allow supply cover, it would not have been possible to visit another school. Also, it was much easier to contact the advisory service during the time freed from teaching. Most importantly though, it raised the status of the project. Because it was not vying for time with other responsibilities, it was possible to give full focus to the task in hand. It also raised the status of the project in the eyes of colleagues.

TASK 35

Examining one of your own budget initiatives

Think about a recent initiative you have worked on.

- was it adequately resourced?
- if not, why not?
- did this affect the quality of the outcome?
- how might better resourcing have improved the outcome?

As deputy, you are likely to have an active influence on the SDP. It is therefore important to note the implications of the above case study. You should be thinking carefully about the scope and requirements of the action and development you are expecting and what your staff can realistically achieve with the level of available resourcing. Sometimes budgetary constraints will mean that schools are relying more than they would like on the goodwill of their staff – this can really only be a short-term solution, as time and energy spent on one thing are inevitably taken from another task (often general teaching responsibilities).

———— Spending the budget ————

Spending is rarely a problem, but spending efficiently and effectively can be. Although comparison with last year is a valid component of the budgetary process, the model of linking budgetary planning to school development planning points us to the important issue that we should be continually trying to use the budget to support and achieve the school's objectives. Above, we discussed incremental or historical budgeting on the one hand, and zero-based budgeting on the other.

A more pragmatic and workable approach to budgeting involves some element of rejustification of need, but nevertheless starts from the idea of a base budget. This model accepts that a school (or any other institution) has certain costs that have to be maintained merely to sustain its existence (unavoidable expenditure). As well as the obvious costs of teachers and lunchtime supervisors, school premises costs are also largely fixed (although minimal savings could possibly be made on these through changing suppliers etc.). The remaining budget then has to be managed using a combination of historical factors and zero-based justification.

TASK 36

Base budgeting

Obtain a copy of the budget for this or the last financial year. From this information, calculate what the base budget for your school would be.

Then look at the remaining budget allocation and think about the following issues:

- looking at the relevant year's SDP, is the linkage between strategic planning and the budget evident?

- do you agree with the decisions that were made? If you were involved in the planning, think back over the planning process.

- what alternatives were considered or could/should have been considered?

It is all too common in education to find yourself working within a difficult budgetary constraint. This means that you may be involved in difficult decisions about making cuts, rather than deciding how to spend surplus income. The following case study involved one of our deputies in just such a situation.

CASE STUDY

Making budget decisions

Although we knew that there were rumours of possible budget cuts in the LEA for the forthcoming year and there was uncertainty with regard to changing school status etc., in the summer term things were looking optimistic. We had already invested a high proportion of our budget in additional ancillary support as a priority, and this fitted nicely with government plans for increasing classroom assistance. However, through no fault of our own, due to family relocations, during the autumn term we found ourselves unexpectedly losing quite a few children (c. 5 per cent of our roll). Some movement was anticipated, but this was more than normal.

We started to feel uneasy, and discussion was started with the staff to put a temporary (but ultimately permanent) halt on non-essential spending plans. The 'storm clouds' gathered further when the higher than expected pay awards were announced – although we felt they were more than justified. The final nail in the coffin was the news that our budget allocation for the forthcoming year was static in relation to last year. Although we had a reasonable projected surplus for the current year, maintaining our current level of expenditure would have still taken us into deficit in the forthcoming year. Some hard choices obviously had to be made.

In preliminary discussions with the head, it was obvious that she was thinking in terms of limping through the next year and making as minimal cuts as possible and 'hoping things would improve'. As deputy, I felt very uneasy about this; although at the same time I felt guilty, because what I was thinking would mean several people's lives being affected due to loss of their part-time positions – it also went against my head's wishes. However, I still felt I had to voice my opinion. I urged a longer-term view. We had to make savings now which would work for the next two years (at current levels of pupil numbers and budget totals), so that we wouldn't find ourselves in equally dire straits the same time next year. The morale of the remaining staff would not stand two such severe knocks. There was a danger that parental confidence would be undermined less if the issue were dealt with more thoroughly now.

The next step was discussion with the governors. The head was still putting forward the 'limp through and see what happens' version – which I sympathised with but couldn't back. Several governors, who are involved in financial management in their jobs, straight away questioned this approach and proposed the longer-term plan – indeed it was felt that it would be seen as an illegal or unsustainable plan otherwise. The head conceded that, rationally, more drastic cuts to stabilise for next year were necessary, but that instinctively/humanly she was against it.

Alternatives for the necessary cuts are now being fully explored, which will stabilise the current situation over the next two budgetary periods (as far as it is ever possible to project in a continual climate of change).

TASK 37

Cutting times ... or making the most of what you've got

Look back to Task 36. Using the figures calculated there, imagine your school is facing a cut of 5 per cent for the coming year. Devise two viable alternatives to present to the governing body in order to deal with the crisis.

Using your figures from Task 36, imagine your school were receiving a 5 per cent increase for the coming year (over and above what is expected). What would be the best use of this additional income to raise standards in your school? Again, look at two viable alternatives and link it to school self-evaluation and objectives.

Summary

In conclusion, let us re-emphasise that budgeting is an important tool which, as a manager, you need to understand. It is an on-going constraint on action in many ways, but it does challenge you to think, question, justify, plan, monitor, evaluate – all useful, indeed essential, processes in an effective school. Above all, avoid the mistake of underestimating the most important asset in your school – people's time.

As a deputy head, you are in an important and difficult position in that you are close to the impact of financial decisions on everyday classroom life, as well as having a feel for the overall context. Your advice as a member of the school's senior management team must be informed and helpful if you are to play your full part.

Our intention is that, at the end of this chapter, you will have:

- understood the differences between historical and zero-based budgeting
- lessened your fear of 'big numbers'
- appreciated the relationship between financial planning and planning in other areas (e.g. to achieve quality, to improve curriculum, to deliver continuing professional development)
- begun to bring flexible/creative approaches to budget planning.

chapter fifteen

Personal development

The learning school

How to learn

Pathways to promotion

Summary

As a deputy you are going to give a lot of energy to your post, and you will need to exercise many skills. At first glance, you might see this as a good reason for not getting too involved in giving the time and energy that professional self-development costs. Indeed, you may be placing more emphasis on promoting the professional development of your colleagues – through appraisal or through organising the school's in-service programme – than you are expending on your own development. As a medium- to long-term policy, this is a bad move. Your role is one of the most varied in the school. Ultimately, you may want promotion to headship, but even just to sustain your sharpness in your current role you need to be looking at a variety of updating activities and ways of progressing your skills. Just think about the range of responsibility you have:

- managerial and leadership
- administrative and organisational
- teaching and curriculum
- disciplinary
- perhaps, pastoral.

These break down into a whole variety of subdivisions:

- interpersonal
- technological
- pedagogical
- counselling related
- financial, and so on.

In Chapter 3 we noted some roles that deputies play, and we talked about the fact that too often the deputy has no, or at any rate a very poor, job description. This is not just our impression. Havard – albeit in a small-scale study – researched the jobs of promoted staff in Scottish schools. He found that:

> *Only 14% of promoted staff in primary schools and 26% of those in secondary schools were able to produce job descriptions when asked by the research team ... job descriptions that were produced were relatively undeveloped ... job descriptions were rarely used as working documents to define management tasks.*
>
> (Havard, 1992, no. 57, p. 29, 6 December)

Given that such a situation prevails all too commonly, where does one go to promote professional development for oneself as a deputy?

First, be sure what your job is. In Chapter 3 we suggested that if you are one of those without a (developed) job description you write one. One could go on to suggest that you seek to have your job description formally agreed and ratified by the head and governing body. Armed with this yardstick, you can at least begin to make a sensible start on planning out the kinds of experiences you need to develop your role and career. Revisit Task 8, if you need to do so.

—————— The learning school ——————

The second thing you can do is to consider the following. Professional development, and professional self-development, are not simply a matter of attending a few courses, however relevant. One modern theory of management is that schools or commercial enterprises need to become learning organisations. This is quite a tricky concept to define, but Holly does so by listing what learning organisations do:

> ■ *Learning organisations look to the future by looking to their present.*
>
> ■ *Learning organisations institutionalise reflection-in-action.*
>
> ■ *Learning organisations treat planning and evaluation as learning.*
>
> ■ *Learning organisations pace their learning and development.*
>
> ■ *Learning organisations attend to the new 'disciplines'.*
>
> ■ *Learning organisations learn from themselves.*
>
> ■ *Learning organisations are life-long learners.*
>
> (Bayne-Jardine and Holly, 1994, pp. 132–6)

To these, O'Sullivan adds:

> ■ *Learning organisations use metacognition, that is they learn how to learn.*
>
> (West-Burnham and O'Sullivan, 1998, p. 34)

Learning schools make themselves open to ideas, have an attitude of mind that seeks continual improvement, use a variety of media and means to gain fresh inspiration, and work collaboratively and at all levels to achieve the goals of learning that they set themselves. To put it negatively, they are schools that have abandoned the fruitless clinging to yesterday's solutions in the hope that these will solve tomorrow's problems. Cartoon character Charlie Brown once summed up this attitude in words something like this:

> *I'm an optimist – I still hope that yesterday will get better.*

But to be successful learning schools need learning staff. Peter Senge, the great guru of learning organisations, puts it thus:

> *There are positive actions that can be taken to create a climate that encourages personal vision. The most direct is for leaders who have a sense of vision to communicate that in such a way that others are encouraged to share their visions. This is the art of visionary leadership – how shared visions are built from personal visions.*
>
> (Senge, 1990, p. 212)

But Senge also, in the present political climate, gives us a timely warning about these visions:

> *There are two fundamental sources of energy that can motivate organisations: fear and aspiration. The power of fear underlies negative visions. The power of aspiration drives positive visions. Fear can produce extraordinary changes in short periods, but aspiration endures as a source of learning and growth.*
>
> (Senge, 1990, p. 225)

Learning, then, is not something just for individuals – it is something that needs to be taken on board by every member of the school community as part of community culture. It is not about attending courses, though this may feature as a means of gaining new skills to contribute to the learning process, it is about attitudes and about developing the vision for the institution. It is about learning continually, and about seeing every situation as a learning situation. It is about reflection on events to draw learning from them, and even about pondering on the reflection itself to understand the learning process. This is the context in which self-development must take place if it is to be fully productive.

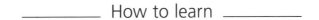

How to learn

With these, perhaps unusual, thoughts in mind, we ask you now to reflect on the kinds of learning on offer to a deputy head wanting to further his or her skills and career. In this section we shall look at some means of learning to further the deputy in the current role. In the next we shall look at pathways to promotion.

Courses (non-validated)

Most educationists contemplating professional self-development instantly think: what courses can I attend?

By courses we mean a series of talks over time on a specific topic. There is nothing wrong with courses. The problem is that they can be blunt instruments. A course covers a topic with broad sweeps, and is aimed at a group of people with disparate learning needs. The teaching methods are likely to be didactic rather than individualised. Courses are useful as a means for updating, for meeting others in the same field, for making contacts, and for getting a 'feel' for other schools' practice – or for being briefed, for example on Local Education Authority policy. The rule is: expect from them only what they can deliver. Before deciding on a course, check that the content is what you want and that the price is cost effective against the likely learning gains. Courses from the 'big-name providers' who spend a great deal of money on advertising may not be the best. Remember, too, who ultimately pays for the advertising!

Conferences

By conferences the intention is to indicate one-day events with major experts in the field as speakers. These are often very costly, but are they cost effective? Like courses, they can provide contacts with other people in the field; the difference is that the conference may be national and the course more local in nature. Conferences are more likely than courses to be 'at the cutting edge' of thinking. As a deputy, it is important for you to keep in touch with the best thinking available in order to help you develop the vision for the school, not simply follow the trend.

Accredited courses and qualifications

For a deputy these are likely to be either at master's degree level (MA, MBA, MEd) or the newer taught doctorates (usually EdD) for those who already have a master's degree. These courses may be delivered mainly through lectures and tutorials, or they may be substantially by distance learning. The choice is the candidate's but it is important to recognise – before opting for one or the other – the extent of your skills in such areas as research methods.

Generally, for the competent researcher, distance courses give the student more flexibility. However, even this is a generalisation, and you may need to investigate the degree of flexibility on offer. For example, at the time of writing, the distance learning MBA at Leicester University's Education Management and Development Unit (EMDU) allows students to set their own timescales within some overall guidance; by contrast, the Open University's MA in Educational Management is very inflexible.

If you have problems working alone or to less strict deadlines, then taught courses may be more suitable for you. This kind of course is designed to give plenty of management knowledge, but also to provide workplace opportunities to carry out small-scale investigations around themes such as personnel management, financial management and so on. The university of Lincolnshire and Humberside is typical of a provider of this kind of course and has a sound national and international reputation. Accredited courses are part of a higher degree marketplace, and you should shop around for what suits your need best.

Reflective practice

Despite the apparent emphasis so far in this section on externally delivered courses, that approach is not always the best. Self-help groups, informally established, can be useful. Thus several deputies might opt to form a group to reflect on their practice, perhaps meeting at each school in turn, or maybe even in their own homes. The aim of the meetings would be to reflect on the problems that they share. Perhaps each meeting would take a pre-determined theme, such as timetabling or new financial arrangements, as its purpose.

In-house reflection

In keeping with the concept of the learning organisation, holders of promoted posts in a school might form a thinktank group to explore ways of producing better collective management.

The reflective log

A useful stand-alone activity is the reflective log or professional journal. This is only of value if it transcends the mere diary. There has to be insightful analysis and reflection on the events recorded, which may be critical incidents, narratives of particular key issues, or even responses to professional reading. To keep such a journal for a period is very instructive and can be the basis of important self-learning. The method epitomises the metacognition approach: reflecting on *how* you learn, not just *what* you learn.

Diary analysis

One useful activity that can be carried out occasionally is to go back over your professional diary. By coding the kinds of activities you undertake (A for administration; C for curriculum-related items; P for public relations activities, and so on) and recording how much time is spent on each, you can check the extent to which your job matches your job description and get some kind of feel for the areas of training that you need to match with what you actually do. So if your diary shows that you spent 40 per cent of your time on attending or chairing committees and 35 per cent on teaching, clearly you need to sustain your training in these areas, while you may feel that you can cope with the 5 per cent of time you are asked to give to public relations.

Observation and peer learning

Throughout this text we have suggested that systematic observation of others is a useful learning tool. You can use the observations you make as part of your curriculum monitoring, or in your role as a mentor for example, as ways of reflecting on practice. Paired observation between peers is a good way to learn. Each watches the other at work, and then they compare notes and impressions. Your own mentor could operate with you in this way.

Personal appraisal

Appraisal and preparing for appraisal are useful tools for reflecting on your own learning. This process forces the issue of taking a long, objective look not only at what you are doing but at how effectively you are doing it.

Professional reading and updating

Even if you do not follow a course of study, such as a higher degree course, you should put some time aside on a systematic basis for keeping up to date through your own reading. This does not mean tackling heavy theoretical tomes, but you should keep in touch with developments through the education press (*Times Educational Supplement* and the education pages of other broadsheet newspapers); and you should take the journal of your particular curriculum association (e.g. the Geographical Association or the Association for Science Education).

We would also recommend that you join the College of Teachers, which has a generalist interest in pedagogy, the process of teaching that underpins everything that happens in schools. If the management process interests you then you could join BEMAS, the British Education Management and Administration Society. Your union will also send out professional literature.

Summary

All the methods listed above contribute to your personal development. Each is valuable in its way. What you have to do is to build yourself a package of activities that fits into the time you have available and that meets your personal needs. A word of warning: it is not permissible to say 'I don't have any time'. If you don't have time to develop professionally you are giving too much time to other things. You have – throughout your professional life – to carve out some small opportunities to grow and progress. It is a biological fact: you either evolve (into a better deputy, into a head) or you prepare for extinction.

Finally in this section, undertake Task 38. This asks you to put together your personal self-development package for the immediate future in your current role as a deputy head. When you have done this you can move on to look at preparation for headship through the National Professional Qualification for Headship (NPQH) route.

TASK 38

Organising your personal professional development programme

The purpose of this Task is to audit your professional development needs. Take some time to work over your professional diary and your job description. First, decide:

■ To what activities are you required to devote most time?

(The headings that follow are designed only to start you thinking, you may add many others!)

Teaching	Curriculum	Pastoral
Examinations	Statistics	Quality control
Finance	Public relations	Attending meetings
Discipline	Media	Chairing meetings
Staff appointments	Timetables	Administration
Leadership	Innovation	Governors

■ Now you need to examine the list you have produced. It will require scrutiny against questions such as:

what does my analysis tell me about the job I actually do?

what skills are implicit in it?

which of these skills do I have?

which should I be improving?

what should I be doing that is not represented here?

what skills are implicit in these omissions?

what is the total list of skills towards which I should be working?

what do I do well or reasonably well?

what things do I do less well?

so what is my prioritised list of things in which I need some training?

■ Having established your training priorities, seek out some training opportunities and make a training plan based on your responses to this Task. Keep to it!

———— Pathways to promotion ————

In contrast to self-directed and self-chosen programmes of in-service training for deputy heads, the Government has put in place an 'official' route for training towards headship: the NPQH. In its own words:

> *the NPQH provides a rigorous, high-quality leadership and management qualification designed specifically to prepare aspiring head teachers for their roles as professional leaders of schools. The practical, professional training provided draws on the best leadership and management practice from inside and outside*
>
> *cont.*

> *education. It is sufficiently flexible to respond quickly to emerging national policy and initiatives, including acting as a key route for disseminating the findings of the Standards and Effectiveness Unit.*

Like most Government initiatives, this has laudable purposes, but those purposes fall within pre-conceived standards of performance. The scheme will not be described in detail here because such information has a tendency to date. At present, the scheme is offered in two versions:

- a 'taught' version operating under the control of local training and development centres
- a supported open learning (SOL) version, using materials and support arrangements developed by a SOL provider.

Clearly, aspiring heads have little option but to opt to undertake this study – even if they decide they also want to gain a master's or similar qualification from a higher education institution as well. Potential candidates need to consult their own Local Education Authorities about support for the course.

We asked a deputy with experience of both the 'taught' version and the SOL version of NPQH to make some assessment of the course. Below we quote from his assessment.

CASE STUDY

NPQH

There have been mixed reactions and complaints by many about the principles of an NPQH and the demands made by it, especially about the increased workload, and the fact that it is an additional burden when being a deputy is already a job and a half.

Personally, I have found it quite flexible, and it certainly encourages you to reflect upon situations and responsibilities. It legitimises putting time aside for thinking and study: a luxury. It has helped me to approach the head and suggest initiatives in the school.

I would sum up the methods of study like this:

> SOL: the timespan for each unit is much longer than in the training centre system. You undertake much more study and provide much more written evidence, as that is the means of communication with your tutor/mentor. You

can contact the tutor by phone; and advice is focused on personal need. The longer timespan also means that you have more 'thinking time'. You have personal control over when you work, so it is less disruptive.

Training Centre: the written workload is much lighter, but the timespan more pressured. The big advantage is in meeting with others in the same situation as yourself. But the pressure of time made it more of a snapshot process. There was less concern with the theoretical underpinning, and more on pragmatism and anecdote.

Overall: I would rate this a beneficial experience. It is also fairer than the previous *ad hoc* systems which paved the road to headships. The framework ensures consistency, yet it is more flexible and context responsive than some people give it credit for.

Whatever training you choose to undertake, what is important is not to lose sight of being a continuous learner and, when your time comes, to run a learning school.

 Summary

Our intention is that, at the end of this chapter, you will have:

- understood the concept of the learning school
- appreciated your own learning needs
- analysed some ways in which you can carry forward your own learning
- formulated a plan for your own continuing professional development
- considered the next step in your career.

Tailpiece

This book has been directed at improving your immediate ability to obtain a post as a deputy head, and then to function effectively and skilfully in that post. As a postscript to the book we asked some deputies to brainstorm what, for them, were the key questions about their impending or actual role. In what follows we draw their questions together and try to answer them in the light of the messages that have been conveyed in this book.

1 Why do I want this job?

Only you can answer this question. It may be for money, power or ambition. It may be because you like a challenge or need a change of role to refresh your professionalism. Most people will have a combination of reasons for moving on to be a deputy. Of those given, the most dangerous is power. Those who seek promotion for power's sake are often the least successful leaders who are most likely to alienate their staffs. Ambition, by contrast, is a legitimate aspiration, even if it is given a bad press by the unambitious. Provided that you know that much of your motivation is coloured by a genuine desire to lead effective education for the good of students, you probably won't be too wide of the mark.

2 How do I feel about 'crossing the line'?

Becoming a deputy is a watershed. You will be a significant part of the management team, and to some at least among your staff you will have crossed the line from 'us' to 'them'. Initially, this will lead to a feeling of alienation or isolation. But these feelings soon pass, as you become part of a new set of groups inside and outside the school. What is important is not to lose empathy with the grassroots feelings of staff. Keep up your friendships with classroom teachers (maybe from other schools), read their views in the *Times Educational Supplement* or the union journals, know how they think. These are important intelligence activities for an effective manager.

———— 3   Have I the right qualities? ————

If you don't have the right qualities, you can probably develop them provided that you are sufficiently reflective in your approach to the role. But what are these qualities? In this book we have identified three, perhaps, as over-arching. They are diplomacy, resilience and insight.

———— 4   Will I lose touch with ———— the classroom?

Inevitably, you will stop being a full-time classroom teacher or, if you are in a small primary school, you will have to be a classroom teacher *plus*. Everyone who works in education management, or in teacher training, or in the academic education world has this dilemma. We each reach our own solution. A personal answer for the author has been always to insist on teaching some part of a timetable, however small. You will have to develop your own solution, but if your innermost feeling is 'Thank God I no longer have to teach', you were probably in the wrong job to start with. You were perhaps not a great teacher and you may not be a great manager either.

———— 5   How can I be expert ———— at everything?

You can't. But you will have experts on your staff. You can learn a lot about many things and you can find out a great deal if you develop the tools. However, you need to learn to trust others who have genuine expertise and to facilitate their ideas. That is an important leadership skill. Real experts will not mind your lack of deep knowledge provided that you understand the broad principles, you are willing to learn, and you trust their judgements. If your in-house 'expert' is actually lacking in expertise, you may have to enlist outside help to guide the school on that issue. The quality of your judgement is what is crucial.

———— 6 What are the key concepts that ———— should guide me in this role?

This book has hinted that there are three concepts without which the deputy will flounder. They are:

- developing priorities
- time management
- delegation.

No manager can do everything, and some tasks are more important than others. (We have dealt in the text with the difference between important and urgent jobs.) You must develop a system of working that prioritises tasks and makes you proactive. The bane of the teaching profession is reactivity. The only destination at the end of that route is a deep pit.

If you prioritise well, then you can target and control your time more effectively. You have to learn to be ruthless about this. Yet, at the same time, you must develop a sense of calm and the quality of always having time to listen to people.

One useful tool is to delegate. That does not mean shedding the whole of your job to someone else. It does mean ensuring that individuals take responsibility for delivering against tasks, targets and timescales that are legitimately part of their duties, leaving you to co-ordinate the efforts of the many.

———— 7 What are the main pitfalls? ————

There are plenty of pitfalls, but the most obvious for the rooky deputy head is to fall into the trap of commanding rather than leading. Innovation requires conviction in the hearts and minds of staff. They will only follow you over the barricades into the no-man's-land of innovation if they want to be with you and identify with you, and if they are persuaded that the goal is worth the risk. This can be a hard business – hence the need for resilience.

———— 8 How can I cope with change when ———— all about me are resisting it?

It is important not to develop a mindset assuming that every decision is a battle and every innovation a lonesome trek. Use persuasion, logic, incentive or whatever it takes to win people over. But the best approach is often not full frontal, that is, a staff meeting, a committee, a vote on a stark choice. Divide people into interest groups, win over one at a time, link favoured ideas with less favoured ones as part of a single package. In fact, use some intelligence. Work incrementally. Don't expect miracles. Never lose sight of the goal. Expect to reach it.

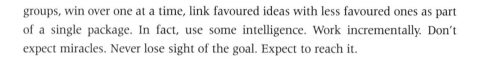

9 Will I cope with the pressure?

Some people don't, but most do. There are probably three things that increase your chances significantly. First, a firm belief in the values that you hold and advocate; this can serve as a rock on the days when things don't progress well. Second, total integrity; know that everything you do is correctly handled and in the best interests of students and staff. Third, have your own ways of relieving your stress away from the workplace: keeping a set hour every evening for your own interests, blasting your frustrations with a hard game of golf or rugby, treating yourself to a favourite tipple on a Friday, going to the cinema – whatever your particular release strategy might be.

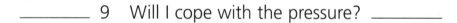

10 What can I do to prepare or improve?

You have done the most important thing – you have read this book! Now all you need is to put the advice into practice and to develop a reflective way of working.

References

Bayne-Jardine, C. and Holly, P. (1994) *Developing Quality Schools*, London: Falmer Press.

Belbin, Meredith (1993) *Team Roles at Work*, London: Heinemann.

Bennis, W. and Nanus, B. (1985) *Leaders*, New York: Harper & Row.

Boyett, I. and Findlay, D. (1995) 'An English case of educational entrepreneurship'. *International Studies in Educational Administration*, **23**(2) 54–67.

Bradley, Michael (1999) 'Re-thinking the way we timetable our schools', *Principal Matters*, **10**(3) 5–8, January.

Champy, James (1995) *Reengineering Management*, London: HarperBusiness.

Covey, Stephen (1992) *The Seven Habits of Highly Effective People*, New York: Simon & Schuster.

Davies, B. and Ellison, L. (1997) *School Leadership for the Twenty-first Century*, London: Routledge.

DFE (1995) *Governing Bodies and Effective Schools*, London: Department for Education.

Duigan, P. (1996) 'Authentic Leadership' key-note address at the ACEA Annual Conference 'Leaders in Education in the Third Millennium' 18 May 1996.

Fidler, B. and Cooper, R. (1987) *Staff Appraisal in Schools and Colleges*, Harlow: BEMAS/Longman.

Harrison, M. and Gill, S. (1992) *Primary School Management*, London: Heinemann.

Havard, J.E.A. (1992) 'Developing school managers', *Studies in Educational Administration*, p. 29.

Hodgson, Jane (1996) *Thinking on Your Feet in Negotiations*, London: Pitman.

Kerry, Trevor (1998) *Questioning and Explaining in Classrooms*, London: Hodder & Stoughton.

Kerry, Trevor (1999) 'The future for schools and schools for the future', *Education Today*, **49**(1) 3–16.

Lowe, B. (1998) 'The bolt-on appendage', *Primary School Manager*, March/April, pp. 18–20.

Middleton, Michael (1999) 'Re-thinking the way we timetable our schools', *Principal Matters*, Vol. 10.3, pp. 5–8, January.

Senge, Peter (1990) *The Fifth Discipline: the Art and Practice of the Learning Organisation*, London: Century Business.

REFERENCES

Watson, K., Modgil, C. and Modgil, S. (1997) *Educational Dilemmas: Debate and Diversity, Vol. 1: Teachers, Teacher Education and Training*, London: Cassell.

West-Burnham, J. and O'Sullivan, F. (1998) *Leadership and Professional Development in Schools*, London: Financial Times/Pitman.

Index